KIDS' LETTERS TO
PRESIDENT OBAMA

BALLANTINE BOOKS

New York

Kids' Letters To

PRESIDENT

OBAMA

EDITED BY

Bill Adler and

Bill Adler, Jr.

Published in the United States by Ballantine Books,
an imprint of The Random House Publishing Group,
a division of Random House, Inc., New York.

BALLANTINE and colophon are registered
trademarks of Random House, Inc.

LIBRARY OF CONGRESS CATALOGING-IN-PUBLICATION DATA
Kids' letters to President Obama / edited by Bill Adler and Bill Adler, Jr.

p.   cm.

ISBN 978-0-345-51712-8 (hardcover : alk. paper)
1. Obama, Barack—Correspondence.   2. Children—United
States—Correspondence.   3. American letters.   4. Children's writings,
American.   I. Adler, Bill.   II. Adler, Bill.

E908.A4 2009b
973.932092—dc22   2009005869

Printed in the United States of America
on acid-free paper

www.ballantinebooks.com

2 4 6 8 9 7 5 3 1

FIRST EDITION

To Karen, Claire, Madeleine, and Amanda,

who get to see such wonderful changes

CONTENTS

★

Forty-six years ago I edited *Kids' Letters to President Kennedy,* who was, until now, the American president most admired by children. Without the Internet, without email, faxes, or even easily available photocopiers, there was only one way to compile a book like this: I had to go to the White House.

Can you imagine calling the White House now, in 2009, and asking if you could sit in the mailroom for a day or two to go through the letters they received from children for a book you wanted to compile? But that's exactly what I did. I called the White House. It was a vastly different world back then. When I called I was put through to the president's press secretary, Pierre Salinger, who thought that *Kids' Letters to President Kennedy* was a terrific idea. "Come on down," he said.

When I arrived at the White House, a marine guard asked for identification. Not being a licensed driver, all I had was a photostat, as they were called, of my army discharge paper. That was good enough and I was ushered into the White House mailroom.

Lacking a portable scanner, digital camera, or any instrument other than a pen and paper, I had to copy each letter by hand. It was slow going, as you can imagine, so at 6:00 pm when the White House mailroom was about to close, I still had hours of transcribing to do. I asked if I could stay to continue my work. "Yes" was the answer. "Just turn out the light when you're done."

And that's how *Kids' Letters to President Kennedy* was done.

While we had all the speed and convenience of technology to help us put together *Kids' Letters to President Obama,* I think one thing is still very much the same: the smart, funny, idealistic, and ingenious kids who are the authors. That shines through in their letters to the president just as brightly now as it did in 1962.

Bill Adler, Sr.
New York, N.Y.

. . . . .

I've written or edited more than twenty books and I can't think of one that has brought me as much joy as *Kids' Letters to President Obama.* The sheer outpouring of excitement, hope, and inspiration is overwhelming. From concerns about littering and pollution to wondering what it will be like to be the first African American President; from suggestions on how to care for a dog in the White House to ideas for making America a better place; telling the president what their own life is like, these letters touch the mind and the heart. The thoughtfulness and genuineness in these children's minds is evident in their letters.

You'll also note that some of the kids' letters include their spelling mistakes, while others, even from very young children, are error-free. Our general rule was to present the letter with the child's inventive spelling preserved; however, if the parents had already fixed the kids' mistakes or took down the letter from the child's dictation, then the letter is presented as edited. At the back of this book you will find a glossary just in case you need help with the translation from kids' English to standard English.

The ideas, of course, are completely the kids' own. They love to suggest how to make the world better. Some of the children's ideas may seem a bit goofy (but then again so are some of the ideas that adults have about trying to run our government); some of these ideas are, well, let's just say less than practical. But some are brilliant! President Obama may want to put *Kids' Letters to President Obama* by his night table for inspiration and reference.

I hope you enjoy reading *Kids' Letters to President Obama,* and I hope that this book brings a smile to your face, as it did to mine. In a way, this book has been forty-six years in the making. I know that President Kennedy would have been proud to have read it.

Bill Adler, Jr.
Washington, D.C.

KIDS' LETTERS TO
PRESIDENT OBAMA

CHAPTER 1

WOW, You're the President! You ROCK!!!

⭐

Almost every letter sent to President Obama included an expression of congratulations. But some went beyond that to tell, often in the most charming and enthusiastic way, what that unique moment in history meant to that child.

Most of these kids have only known one president in their lifetime before Barack Obama, so they don't have the sense of history that comes with being older and having so many more memories of the past. Nor have they studied much, if anything, of past presidents in school. Still, many of these young correspondents seem to have grasped as thoroughly as any adult the meaning of Barack Obama's unprecedented victory on election night. And we have no doubt that they will all remember for the rest of their lives what they were doing on the night of November 4, 2008.

Dear President Obama,

I think it is awesome to be our new President because I think you are going to make a ton of smart choices. I think you will be our goodest President.

When I grow up, I want to be President too. I think it would be fun and helpful to other people. I think I would be good at being a President because I help people move things around, give people the answers to questions they want to know, and when people are lonely, I play with them.

Gabriel, age 7
Bothell, WA

Dear President Obama,

So your dad is from Kenya. So am I. HOW EXCITING. Did you know that Kenya had a national holiday because you kind of came from Kenya?

It would be so cool if I had a playdate with your daughters. How exciting would that be!

You are going to be a terrific, trying-hard president. Go ahead and do your job. Bye!!

Yours truly,
Doris, age 9
Evanston, IL

Dear President Obama,

Great your president now! Did you know my mom cried when you won? I wrote your name on my head and went to bed so you would have good luck. Don't walk under any ladders or spill any salt.

I think that you will be a great President because you have a great family. I wish I could live in the White House with all the cool stuff. I heard you can't go to your barber any more. He has to come to you.

President Obama, you are a great man. I hope you lower gas prices and stop global warming. This is one of the biggest elections ever. I think that this is history. I will be able to tell my kids about this.

Sincerely,
Christian

Christian, age 10
Evanston, IL

Dear Mr. Obama,

My mom and dad woke me up in the middle of the night to see your acceptance speech on TV. It is an important time in history because you're the first black president. I am black and my brother is black, but my mom and dad are white. Now I know I can be a president, too!

>Sincerely,
>Corey, age 9
>Baltimore, MD

Dear President Obama,

Before you were elected I put you on my dream board!! That is a board that you put something you want on it!!! When I knew you were president, I called my neighbors, but they did not answer so I yelled "Obama Won" on their answering machines.

>Thank you
>For being
>Our President!!

>Sincerely,
>Sofía, age 9
>Portland, OR

Dear Barack Obama,

Congratulations for winning the election. I am so happy for you. My momma voted for you. I didn't want you to be our president just because you were black, I wanted you to be our president because you looked like a nice guy. And your speech was good.

Obama, let me tell you what I want to be in the future. I want to be a doctor and a lawyer so that I can help people when they are hurt. And if somebody goes to jail I can help them out. I love to help people when they are hurt or if they fall or something.

Obama, can I come to the White House and meet you? I am a big fan, and your daughters are cute, and by the way, I am a girl. Obama, I really do want to come to the White House just to meet you and your family.

Thank you for everything, Obama. I am so happy that you are my president and you are the first black president. I am black, too.

Sincerely,
Jasmine, age 12
Anderson, S.C.

Dear President Obama,

Congratulations on winning the White House. You're the best president in the world.
You ROCK!!!

Dylan, age 7, and
Tessie, age 5
Bethesda, MD

Dear

Dear presindet Oboma,
good luck on your NecxT
job. Has thar bin eney changis.

Congojalashens for being are
presedent. Oboma. How is eure
Thing going What wus your
child hod like. I'm six in a half.
My Birther is march 6. The day
you got The moste votes. The

NecxT morning I saw you In
The nowday* From Katie
To brocoe bama.

* Newsday is a paper.

Katie, age 6½
Northport, N.Y.

Dear President Obama,

It is such an amazing and extraordinary honor to be alive for such a revolutionary experience in my lifetime. I remember the months of your candidacy. All the children at my school wanted you to win so badly. The night of November 4, at 8:00 pm, I remember flipping through channels. At that moment, my dad ran into the room yelling "Obama won!" I was so happy. My father told me that he never thought in his lifetime that our nation will have an African American president. It's not even about race. It's that our nation can overcome the discrimination and prejudice. It's the fact we can agree to make a better place.

Thank you for the assurance that you can bring our nation's best possible future.

Jasmine, age 12
Sacramento, CA

Dear President Obama,

I would like to start off by saying congratulations on winning the presidency. Even though I was originally a Clinton fan, I am very excited that you are my president. Although I am only a thirteen year old girl living in rural Vermont, I am aware of the world around me. Over the last eight years I have grown more and more annoyed with the current condition that American is in. I trust that you will do your best to get us out of this slump and back on track.

Sincerely,
Leah, age 13
Randolph, VT

Dear President Obama,

Hello, my name is Andrew and I am 10 years old. I live in Fargo, North Dakota and was able to see you when you visited our city. My dad and I stood in line for two hours to get tickets and even longer when we went to see you. But it was worth it—I think you waved at me! I voted for you in my fourth grade class mock-election, but you didn't win. I was so happy that you won the real election and now lead America.

I know my life will be better because you are president. I would like you to help stop global warming and hope you bring back the electric car. I would like it if you could make a law against littering in the ocean. I want the war in Iraq to stop and hope you can do something about that. It would be good if you could help doctors make cures for some of the diseases.

Please make the world a better place.

Sincerely,
Andrew, age 10
Fargo, N.D.

Dear President Obama,

Congratulations on winning the election in November. My parents voted for McCain. If I could vote, I would have voted for you, but I'm only 12 years old and I have to be 18 to be able to vote for president.

I know you will bring change all around the world. You will be a very good president.

Sincerely,
♥ Casey ♥, age 12
Anderson, S.C.

Dear barack,

Congraltans for being President! Soon you are going to the wite house. You are the first African-American isn't that great? I'm so excited for you to get in to the wite house. I hope you make good laws. My mom voted for you. If you need me here is my phone numbr. 301-XXX-XXXX.

Sincerely,
Evelyn, age 6½
Bethesda, MD

The next 3 letters are from a brother and 2 younger sisters. Their father notes that they spent a "long time writing, to get the letters just right."

DeaR PRESIDont Obama,

I wish you beat
every PRESIDeNt IN the
UNIVeRSe.
MeRRY GRISTNMas.
I Love you.

Love,
ReeM

5YeARS OLD

Reem, age 5
Chicago, IL

Dear President Barack Obama,

Deena writes:
WOW! We're so happy you are president! Hope you have a good time at the White House. Sorry to hear to your grandmother died, but it happens.

Samir writes:
Are you excited to meet all of the famous world leaders? I'd be! Wait, one more thing. Can you invite a few kids to the White House? I'd love for you to invite me because I'm smart, I know how to play basketball, and I can be nice to your daughters because I have 5 sisters!

> Respectfully yours,
> Samir, age 9, and
> Deena, age 6
> Chicago, IL

Dear President Obama,

Congratulations on becoming our first Afro-American President. I am so proud of you and your accomplishments. You remind me of my Daddy, just like yourself he also is an honest, hard-working man that puts his family first. What advice can you give me so that one day when I grow up, I can become the first Afro-American female President?

> Kyra, age 8
> Gold River, CA

Dear President Obama,

You have provided an inspiration to me that no one else ever has. Because of you I honestly believe anything is possible if you put your mind to it and never give up. Because of your run for the White House, I've actually wanted to follow politics and know what is going on, whether it's the primary elections or the actual election between you and Senator McCain. I wouldn't even have started watching politics if it wasn't for you.

One thing I have also learned is how being level-headed, even in the most pressuring situations, is important. Another thing I have learned from your speeches is that everyone is important, no matter where they are from or what the color of their skin is, and that everyone should have an equal chance. Also because of you I learned how lucky I am and I have become much more appreciative of everything I have. Thanks to you I will never give up my love of politics, my love to help others. You have shown me that it is possible to bring a nation together. But most importantly, you have given me inspiration to care more about this country, and one day I also hope to become the President and be as inspirational as you. I have become a better person because of you. So I thank you, President Obama, for everything you have done for me.

Anton, age 13
Los Angeles, CA

Dear President Obama,

I can't believe I am sitting down with my laptop, and actually writing these words to you. I can remember how I was on November 4th, sitting with my eyes glued to the television screen, watching CNN as I tried not to hyperventilate. I remember whooping and cheering as we saw your electoral votes surpass 270, and Senator John McCain made his concession speech. It was the happiest day of 2008, a day filled with anticipation, triumph, an overwhelming sense of unity and more than anything—hope.

At this moment, nothing seems more at stake than our futures, with the failing global economy and unraveling ecological system, with the conflicts and violence, which are occurring as I type these words. Me and my friends are of every race, religion and class. In my heart I know that it's our God-given right to be able to go in pursuit of our happiness and to live, not just the American Dream, but what I'm sure is the dream of every child alive in the world today.

Sometimes when hope seemed lost, I would conjure in my minds the words you have spoken: "We know that the battle ahead will be long, but always remember that nothing can stand in the way of billions of voices calling for change . . . We have been asked, all of us, for a reality check. We have been warned against giving the people of this nation false hope, but in the unlikely story that is America, there has never been anything false about hope."

You have given us hope, and that's more than we have had from a leader in a long time. But as you have said so many times yourself, there is work to be done. I know that change has not happened, but we are closer to it than we have been in the past eight years. And Mr. President, I feel alive in my anticipation of the change you promise to bring to Washington, the United States and the world in these next four years.

Sincerely,
Ritah, age 13
Bangkok, Thailand

Dear President Obama,

As a Black female, I'm going to try to be the first woman president, and the first Black woman president at that—that is, if no one beats me to it.

If we could meet face to face I would be so honored. In a couple of years you will be a legend. One day I will be able to tell my children and grandchildren, "The first Black president was elected."

Sincerely,
Kiana, age 12
Anderson, S.C.

Dear President Obama,

The good news is that my whole family voted for you. Even though my grandma usually votes for the Republican party, she changed her mind after she heard your amazing speeches.

I try to watch the news as much as possible now because of the changes in the United States right now.

Something I have noticed is that the economy is getting very bad right now. People are losing their jobs and are not able to pay for the things they need like food and clothes. Because of the changes you promised, my family was very into the election, and I was, too.

I think you being president will make a big change in the world and everything will be better. So congratulations on being elected president!

Sincerely,
Blake, age 11
West Linn, OR

Dear President Barack Obama,

Congrats on becoming our first African American President. You will make a great president and great leader. Sorry about your grandmother dying right before you won the election. But I know while she is in heaven that she is proud of her grandson for having such a great spirit and for becoming so successful.

Sincerely,
Da'chelle, age 12
Philadelphia, PA

Brandon, age 8
Austin, TX

Dear President Obama,

I remember a day in 2004 that is significant to me. My family was sitting around the TV watching the Democratic National Convention. This was the day that you made your speech for Senator John Kerry, supporting his run for presidency against President Bush. After your speech, my mom stood up and looked at the rest of the family. She told us that she had just heard the voice of the next president. How exciting that four years later, her prediction would finally come true! Congratulations on your monumental success! I believe that you will be able to pull this country out of our recent slump. I look forward to having the chance to vote for your return to office in four years.

Sincerely,
Robert, age 15
Pagosa Springs, CO

Dear President Obama:

The evening of the election we all gathered around the television and watched the Election 2008 special. It was a school night, but my parents let me stay up late because this wasn't just any school night. This was Election Night! History in the making, my parents kept saying, reminding me that I'm biracial, too. Oh, one funny thing: My grandmother is Korean and my dad is American, and sometimes their different views of the world end up in shouting matches. But that night the whole house was quiet until the official announcement came. You won! Yay! We jumped up and high-fived.

My mom came home from work the day after the election with a commemorative edition of the Washington Post newspaper. It's wrapped in plastic and hidden away in my closet until I pass it down to my children, long after your presidency has passed. But my memory of Election Night will always be crystal clear in my mind. Someday, when I'm an old man, I'll tell my grandchildren about this amazing moment in American history, and how I was a part of it. Yes, President Obama, you will go down in history as the first African-American President, but I bet you will be remembered more for how you handled all the BIG problems of the day.

Mr. President, I hope that someday you will read my letter.

Sincerely,
Justin, age 10
Springfield, VA

Dear President Obama,

Congratulations on winning the election. McCain didn't have a chance.

The one thing I want to be when I grow up is to be president just like you. It'll be a long road but I can do it.

I think you should start giving out jobs to the poor and apartments for them to live in. My advice is to give out $500 stimulus checks for families that need the money.

Also, give more money for schools, books, field trips, and lunches that are edible.

Sincerely,
Ronnie, age 12
Anderson, S.C.

Dear President Obama,

I'm a 10-year old girl from Brooklyn who had the opportunity to campaign for you in northeast Philadelphia. It was interesting but knocking on doors all day got a teensy bit boring. The one moment my mom said was a real "Obama moment" was when we knocked on a door and a little girl (7 years old) answered who looked lonely. While my mom was talking to her grandma, I started talking to her. We left a few minutes later. When my mom and I were a couple houses up the block, I saw the girl pulling her mom out the door. The mom hesitated then came up to my mom and said, "We just moved so I don't think I'm registered to vote." As my mom was signing her up, I sat down with the girl and we talked some more. I did most of the talking. By the time we left we had gotten to know about each other.

Now, about issues: I am really concerned about global warming. I care strongly for the environment and everything that's in it. I like your idea for new energy sources such as wind and solar. I would like for you to enforce the use of hybrids and even better: bikes.

I'm sincerely worried about what it will bring for the future and not just for us humans but for animals too. I hope you will take this under consideration for I am sure that I'm not the only one concerned about this issue.

From,
Molly, age 10
Brooklyn, N.Y.

P.S. Speaking of animals, I have a suggestion for what breed of dog you should get. A sweet, small, loveable, hypoallergenic dog is a Bichon Frise.

Dear President Obama,

I think you are going to be a so nice President. I think you should fix things in the world to be more fair. You should tell people to stop fighting so others can get along better. I hope you and your little girls have fun in the White House. Nobody is perfect but I think you will be pretty close to perfect. And no matter what, you will be the greatest president ever!

Love,
Reagan, age 6½
Gaithersburg, MD

Dear President Barack Obama,

I really respect you in a way that I can't explain. I really had to beg my dad to vote for you and sit him down and read one of your books and make him listen to your speeches to convince him to vote for you. Some of my friends who voted for John McCain only thought that I wanted to vote for you because you are African American, but that's not true. I voted for you because I think you really care about the people of the United States and will be a great president.

Try to help our country, and give thanks to kids that had to beg and disagree with their parents for you to be president!

Sincerely,
Nikayla, age 11
Newport News, VA

Dear Mr. Obama,

My name is Alexis and I am overwhelmed that you are president. I really, really, really!!! wanted you to win! I am so happy that you're in office on my birthday. You will change everything, right? I have a little bit of advice for some changes. First, will you please make the gas bill go down so it is not hard for so many families. Then please make it not so hard on the moms and dads who are losing their jobs. My aunt already lost hers and she is going to suffer this Christmas. Please save our country.

Yours truly,
Alexis, age 10
Florissant, MO

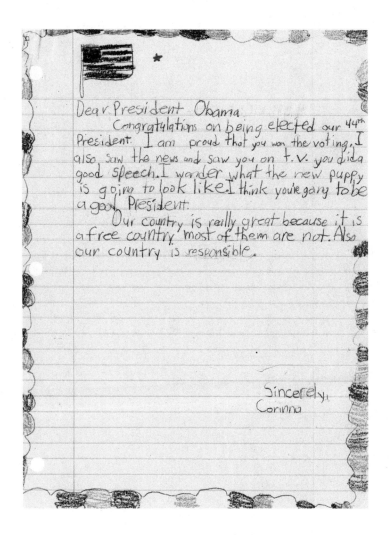

Dear President Obama
    Congratulations on being elected our 44th President. I am proud that you won the voting. I also saw the news and saw you on t.v. you did a good speech. I wonder what the new puppy is going to look like. I think you're going to be a good President.
    Our country is really great because it is a free country most of them are not. Also our country is responsible.

                                    Sincerely,
                                    Corinna

Corinna, age 8
Castaic, CA

Dear Mr. President Obama I just want to say that America made the right choice by electing for our President, and I will tell you why.

I think so because your very cool and handsom. I also think that you make wise disitions. Also an other wise disition is when you helped your community by lowering the gas prises.

I just want to say that you are going to make history in our lifetime because you are the first African American to be our President and I wan't to thankyou for that

Sincerly,
April

April, age 10
Sherman Oaks, CA

Dear President Barack Obama,

I was keeping track of your campaign. This was my first time actually paying attention to a presidential race. I stayed up late at night to hear the announcement of your presidency. I must admit that the final outcome left me in tears. All through the next day in school you were the main topic. I know that you have the most challenging job in the whole country. How will you be able to protect the United States and remain the cool, relaxed person you are?

A believer,
Morgan, age 13
Philadelphia, PA

Dear President Obama,

I really can't find the words to describe the joy I feel typing "Dear President Obama." We did it. We actually did it. Yes we did.

You've probably heard about the whole "Barack Obama inspires young people" phenomenon. I feel that it's true, as I am living proof. "Pre-Obama," I didn't know what was currently happening in our world. I didn't know anything about how our government functioned. But when I heard you talk about our world's problems and that in order to change our ways, we would have to unite as the United States of America—not red states against blue—I came to realize that our country was in desperate need of change, and you were the one to lead us.

So, for the first time, I volunteered at our local phone bank to make your presidency a reality. When I overheard my parents discussing plans to canvass in Nevada for you, I immediately told them that they were crazy to think that they could go without me.

Seeing a single mother with seven children holding a yard sale while their house was in foreclosure really brought home for me that our country was in need of change. While working with all of the politically, economically, and socially diverse people who had literally devoted their lives to campaign for you, I fully realized your power to inspire, and began to think that we could really pull this off.

So thank you. Thank you for inspiring me to participate in something that I truly believe in. You were my motivation; you intrigued me enough to discover this passion and to learn about our country. And thank you for regaining our respect as a country, beginning to fix the many remaining problems, and making America a place that I am proud to be a part of.

We did it,
Lena, age 13
Pacific Palisades, CA

CHAPTER 2

Take My Advice, Mr. President

★

When kids give advice, they don't need to worry about whether there's enough political support for the idea to become a law, or even whether the idea is possible under the laws of physics!

Kids have a refreshingly straightforward approach with the advice they give. If something is wrong, fix it. If someone needs help, help them. There is no "yes, but" that takes into account the cost, the possibility of failure, or the worry that wrongheaded advice might even make the problem worse.

If only we could do everything just as they suggest. Then we would end all warfare on the spot, give everyone a job, and make sure all the litter on earth was picked up.

In the purest sense, and without any self-interest, kids embody Barack Obama's "Yes We Can" philosophy.

Dear President Obama,

I know you have a lot to work on but do you think you could pass a law making chocolate a vegetable in our country? Thank you for considering this.

Sincerely,
Keaton, age 7
Duvall, WA

Dear Mr. Obama,

I hope that you can lower bills and gas prices. Maybe you can make Hummers illegal. I would also like less homework and a shorter school year.

I really hope that the Lego company doesn't need a bailout, but if they do, I hope that you can help them!

Very sincerely,
Anthony, age 9
Kensington, MD

Dear mr. President
I woould like No roads
to have bumps. in
them, because it is
bad for cars to goon
the bumps, thank
you.
Amelie, 6

Amelie, age 6
Acton, MA

Dear Mr. Obama,

Can you un-ban cloning so I can clone myself, and is the moon a part of the United States? Can you make it where people of all ages are able to get a job because some kids don't get allowances?

Are space dinosaurs real? I think not, because for one, it's really unlikely for a dinosaur to be alive and not have to breathe oxygen, but my uncle believes in them.

> Signed,
> A kid,
> Steven, age 11
> St. Louis, MO

Dear President Obama,

My advice is:

1. Be a good president!
2. Sign peace treaties.
3. Last thing: Have a GREAT time being president!

> Sincerely,
> Ariella, age 9
> Chicago, IL

P.S. I want NO war in this world!

Dear President Obama,

My suggestion to solve the economic problem is to give each American citizen $200,000 to spend on whatever they like.

Sincerely,
Nathan, age 12
Sharon, VT

Dear President Obama,

I'm glad that you won for president. I will help you learn to bowl because you don't know how to bowl. The highest score I've ever got was 109 points with bumpers. The highest score without bumpers was 60. I think you will be a better president than George Bush because you have good ideas. George Washington was the first president of the United States of America. My school is named after George Washington's house, Mount Vernon.

Love,
Jon, age 6½
Alexandria, VA

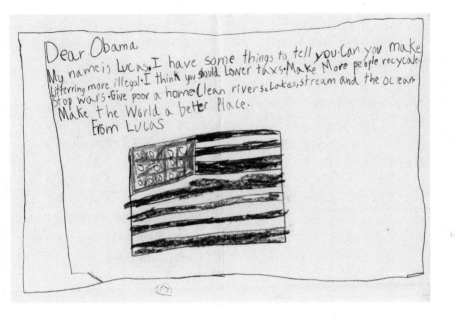

Dear Obama
My name is Lucas. I have some things to tell you. Can you make littering more illegal. I think you should Lower taxs. Make More people recycale. Stop wars. Give poor a home. Clean rivers, Lakes, stream and the ocean. Make the World a better Place.
From Lucas

Lucas, age 8
Austin, TX

Dear President Obama,

We voted for you. We love you! Congratulations! Here's what you should do:

Please take good care of the earth because if you take good care of the earth, the earth will take care of you. (It's a song we sing in school.)

And don't listen to Bush!

Be a leader, not a follower

Don't fight with countries around the world

Please come on vacation with us and bring Joe Biden.

Love,
Leila, age 5½,
and my little brother,
Cyrus, age 3
New Canaan, CT

Mr. Obama,

I have a new idea for a new holiday, First Ladies Day! Do you like the idea?

You know, before you were elected president, I thought you were so cool. I still do!!! You are lucky to be elected president because I know you'll be great!! I have a question for you, were you shocked when you were elected president?

Well, it was great talking to you Mr. Obama!!

Sincerely,
Halle, age 9
St. Charles, MO

Dear President Obama,

There are a few things I would like to tell you. My name is Genevieve and I live in Glendale, California. I am six years old and I play soccer. I hope you will be a kind man. and do gode tings for the conchrey. Pleys make sere are conchrey has cline air. Lastly, I have some advice I would like to give you. I thinke you shod be kind and have kertusy, and show gode respeckt. I enjoyed wrting this letter to you Good luke as President.

From
Genevieve

Genevieve, age 6
Glendale, CA

Dear President Obama,

Can you please be a good President?

Be nice and don't yell.

We want you to recycle like me too. Please help the Earth to be a healthy, nice, planet because it's our home.

Love,
Caleb, age 5, and
Emma, age 7
Essex Junction, VT

Dear President Barack Obama,

My name is Jackson but you can call me Jack for short. It is nice of you to be our new President of the United States of America.

I'm writing to ask if you can change the rule about only those who are born in America could become president. My Dad was born in Haiti and he's a great Dad. I think he will make a great President too! He helps me with my homework, he's always talking about politics, and plus my Mom calls herself the First Lady of the House. I know you grew up in Hawaii. My dad was born in Haiti but he grew up in America. I hope while you are President you will be able to change this law so my Dad can run for President next time. I want a dog too!

I wish you good luck in your new job as President of the United States of America.

From,
Jackson, age 8
Brooklyn, N.Y.

P.S. Write back if you need ideas to change the rule.

Brooklyn twins Olivia and Elijah sent their ideas in two letters:

Dear President Barack Obama,

My name is Olivia. I am eight years old. My family and I voted for you in the election. We are so happy that you won.

I think that the people who voted for you would like you to please stop the war. The way you can handle trying to stop the war may be to make a good compromise that the other people will agree on. Also, please make sure that people who are retired, like my Nana, Grandpa, Grandma and Granddad, can still pay for anything that they need to.

Finally, here is a suggestion that I would like: Please make Pajama Day and a sibling day called Naptime Day when you read, play math games, have an assembly and recess and then naptime and then finally pack up and go home.

Sincerely,
Olivia, age 8
Brooklyn, N.Y.

Dear President Obama,

I am eight years old and I am a twin. I was born in the year 2000 which is the Year of the Dragon. I like math. I already know division and I'm in the third grade.

I want you to please give homes to the homeless and please give the poor money.

Will you please explain to me why did the economy mess up?

On Election Day my sister and I went with our Dad to vote. Daddy let Olivia touch the lever and I pulled the lever to vote for you!

Sincerely,
Elijah, age 8
Brooklyn, N.Y.

Dear Mr. President,

I have a concern about electricity. We are losing it quickly., but I think I have a solution. My friend and I were talking and suddenly had an idea. If you can convert wind and water into electricity, couldn't you use sound to make electricity? Sound is everywhere, especially in our classroom. I can't imagine my teacher encouraging my class to talk—it's like the lights at an opera or concert operating on the music and the cheers.

I wish you the best of luck in your new job, and a very happy term.

Jonah, age 11
Calabasas, CA

Dear Barack obama,
I think you should try to
stop people from littering,
because if people stoped
littering than it would
stop poluting the enviorment.
And it would make people
happier, I hope!
from your Dear friend Emmaline

don't forget
to recicle

Emmaline, age 9
Austin, TX

Dear President Obama,

I would recommend that you try to help people stop drug addiction. To stop it, my only advice is to hold a meeting and talk about it. Once you figure out what to do, go on television and say how it is affecting our country.

The thing I don't like about addiction to drugs is that homeless people buy drugs because they're down and lonely. They can be happy just from their souls . . .

I hope my advice is a help to you and the country. I hope our country can be a healthy, drug-free country where people are happy and believe in themselves.

Sincerely,
Samantha, age 10
Wasilla, AK

Dear Mr. Obama,

You seem very nice. Can you help the country by making people be nice to people they do not like? Can you please, because I hate it when people yell at other people for no good reason. It just makes me feel sad.

Your friend,
Alec, age 9
Florissant, MO

Dear Presedent Obama,

When you become presedent can you make a space hotel because A lot of people want to go to outer space.

love,
Nathaniel

P.S.

My moms from Amarica and my dads from Kenya just like you.

Nathaniel, age 8
Silver Spring, MD

Dear President Obama,

Do you travel for your job or with your family? I think you should travel to places that have been damaged by floods or storms. Then you can bring in supplies to repair the town or city.

Sincerely,
Sean, age 8
Index, WA

Dear President Obama,

Even though I'm just a 4th grader I have some pretty decent ideas on how you can run the country. Increase all school hours by 1 to 2 hours but start school 1 to 2 hours later. (So kids have more time to get ready for school.)

Though you are president, it doesn't mean you can't focus on your private life. But never talk to your children about how you became president or how you're so cool or awesome. You'll be teaching them a horrible lesson of bragging. Plus, they'll get annoyed.

Sincerely,
Lucas, age 9
Takoma Park, MD

Dear President Obama,

I think you should ban gas cars. That might fix global warming problems. Then people can have cars that run off of vegetable oil.

I know you're going to be a good president. I wonder if you always wanted to become president? I also wonder if you were a nerd in school?

I hope you can write back.

Your citizen,
Jay, age 11
Anderson, S.C.

Dear President Obama,

If I was president I would do a lot of things, but I will only tell you five. One, I would make a nursery so poor people would have a place to get better. Two, I would stop fires that can hurt people. Three, I would tell people not to litter a lot. Four, I would save wild animals from hunters. Five, I would say a good speech in front of everyone in the United States of America. That's what I would do if I was president.

Love,
Cameron, age 7
Valley Glen, CA

Dear President Obama,

Why did you want to be president? I mean it's a great job, but, it's a hard job running a country. You have to make rules people like. You have to make them happy. You have to help some people lead a better life. You have to help the poor. How are you sure you are ready to do it all? But I think you are ready to do this. Probably most people think you are ready to do this. Some probably don't.

Some things I would like to tell you is if you realy want to do the job, I would do whatever is perfect for the people. I would keep them happy. I would do whatever is right for people. I'd make rules that are right for everyone and everything. I'd do what's best for the country. I hope you do the best.

Sincerely,
Kyle
age:7

Kyle, age 7
Wheatley Heights, N.Y.

Dear President Obama,

I really want you to give everybody in the whole planet ice cream. And don't forget that you can give us ice cream too. But we should buy it, okay? My favorite kind is vanilla. What's your favorite?

I really liked hearing you on my computer and I'd like to go to the White House some day.

From,
Garrett, age 5
(for 3 more days!)
Albany, OR

Dear Mr. Obama,

The purpose of this letter is to tell you what I'd like to see happen while you're president.

First, please stop the Iraq war as soon as possible. War is bad and it makes us seem like a not very nice country.
Second, please help stop global warming and pollution so the earth is still pretty when your daughters and I grow up.
Third, could you please change the law so that kids age 8 and up can vote. It's our country, too.

Thank you for making Americans believe that we can make America beautiful again.

From,
Roxanne, age 8
Austin, TX

Dear President Obama,

My name is Jaxin but you can call me Jak. So can you do something for me? Can you end the war? Also, can you stop people selling tobacco in stores? Can you give food to the kids in Africa so they can live and play with toys? Can you tell cashiers to ask for an I.D. so people don't get wasted at parties if they're underage?

Sincerely,
Jaxin, age 11
Des Moines, IA

Dear President Obama,

Hello! My name is Natalie and I am writing this letter because I want to share my feelings with you.

The ideas you have given us for our country's future are terrific! But I would like to recommend some ideas that I have. I would like our seas, oceans, ponds, and lakes to be kept clean to save our animals.

I would also like to recommend that we help Europe with some problems that they have. I say this because I have traveled to Europe and the things I experienced there will be with me for the rest of my life. Smoking is allowed at the age of 15 there, and their speed limits I believe are too fast and too dangerous. My family and I were almost in a car accident because of the speed limit being 100 mph!

If I were president, I would help every country, every soul, and every heart that needed someone to be with them in their hardest times. Just to keep peace in this world until the day that I die.

I BELIEVE IN YOU!!!

Sincerely,
Natalie, age 12
Stillwater, OK

Dear President Obama,

Please remember to be peaceful.
Sydney, 6

Sydney, age 6
Gaithersburg, MD

CHAPTER 3

I Have a Few Questions, If You Don't Mind. . . .

★

Kids love to ask questions. What better way to find out the answer to a question than to ask the president of the United States? He has all the answers—at least that's what all these young correspondents think!

Kids aren't shy about asking anything and everything that's on their minds. Just imagine what it would be like if President Obama were to give a press conference for all the kids who wrote in with their questions. That certainly would be entertaining . . . and more revealing than many of the presidential press conferences we've watched over the years.

Of course, even the best educated and most nimble-minded politician would be stumped by some of the questions these kids come up with!

Dear President Obama,

I am very glad that you are president. I do have some questions for you. I would like to start off with asking how are you doing? Are you enjoying all aspects of the White-house? I bet you are. I have been wondering ever since the debates aired, are you friends with John McCain? I was just wondering because during the debates everyone said y'all hated each other. Now the press says you are best friends. I just wanted to get that straight!

Is it true that your daughters get ANYTHING that they want now that you are president? I am thinking that once you become president, you have all the money in the world for anything you want. Are you upset about the press making a big deal about EVERYTHING? I know I sure would be.

I know you will be an awesome president. I am happy for you. Remember that we are always praying for you!

With Love,
Hailee, age 9
Knox City, TX

Dear President Obama,

I wanted to ask you some easy questions. I wanted to ask, could you help get more jobs in Anderson, S.C.? Because so many people are getting kicked out of their house and don't have cars because they don't have a job. I also want to ask how could you make the planet green. Because so many are not recycling to help save the planet. And by making drugs and smoking them, they are making the planet worse off.

I want the White House to try to help people in need. And also, do you like being in the White House?

Sincerely your friend,
JacDamian, age 12
Anderson, S.C.

Dear President Obama,

Are you a Good person or a Bad person? Can you give a job to my mom so she can pay the rent for our house? I wish I could be like you and be a nice person. My family needs money. Do you make money for poor people?

Sincerely,
Jasmine, age 9
Des Moines, IA

Dear Mr. Obama

Obama my name is Beau. I am 8 yers old and I am in seckent grad. I live in Glendayol Calafornya. Now I have to ask you some questions. Do you like fishing? do you have a cat? do you no wat you are gowing to do for the state yet? Now I am gowin to tell you aletal bit about my self. I like Brokle, I like fishing, I like under water Gogmfek and siyents and my faveret holaday is cris mis day that is all I have to say plese rite bak.

From,
Beau

Beau, age 8
Glendale, CA

Dear President Obama,

I hear the White House has its own private golf course, is this true? If you could paint the White House another color, what color would it be? I liked how you addressed your kids in your acceptance speech. My sister and I are about the same ages as Malia and Sasha, so it was cool to see kids just like us stand up on stage after your speech.

Have fun at the golf course!

Sincerely,
Kaley, age 11
Austin, TX

Dear President Obama,

I want to know if you think being president will affect your everyday life, like shopping or going out for a walk? Do you think your friends and family will treat you differently because you are president? I was also wondering, what is your favorite song? And who is your favorite singer?

I hope you have a good time in the White House.

Sincerely,
Mateo, age 9
Silver Spring, MD

Dear President Obama,

I want to ask you and Joe Biden some questions. What will you do about the econimical crisis? Will you help all the companies? Will you lower all the taxes? Will you make the USA go green? Will you stop poverty? And, what will you do about crime? Will you get me Guitar Hero? If so, all that will help the USA!

Sincerely,
Sam, age 8
Washington, D.C.

Dear President Obama,

In school were you a slacker or a good student?

Jessie, age 12
Doylestown, PA

P.S. You're awesome and I'm glad you're President.

Dear President Obama,

I have a few questions for you. Nothing that will affect the world situation, but I was just wondering. . . .

I love shrimp and pineapple pizza. What are your favorite foods?
I am not allergic to anything; not any kind of food or any animals. Are you allergic to anything?

There are a lot more questions I'd like to ask you, but I don't want to bug you. You probably have more important, earth-shattering questions to deal with.

> Malaysia, age 11
> Rochester, N.Y.

Dear President Obama,

My first question is what are you going to do about the stock market? Because, as you can see, a lot of businesses are going out of business. My second question is, do you have an expensive car, because I love cars so much.

> From,
> Avery, age 11
> Valley Village, CA

Dear President Barack Obama:

What is it like having to be guarded all the time? How does it change your life? Do you ever get privacy? I would think you would not like it.

I think you will really change this world. For example, I think you will stop the war in Iraq and not start another war. Everyone in the world needs peace. How will you get all the people to stop wars and to bring peace?

> Sincerely,
> Satya, age 8
> Brooklyn, N.Y.

to: Back Obma

Dear President Barock Obama
I just want to ask you
a few questeons like six
questeons 1. how happy
is your wife? 2. what kined
of dog are you going to
get? 3. how happy are
you going to be when
you get to your new house?
4. oh what cinde of muick
do you like.

love angela

by!

Angela, age 9
Austin, TX

Dear President Obama,

Hi! I am so happy that you won the election. I have some questions for you.

1. Do you ever forget where some of the rooms are in the big White House and get lost?

2. My mom told me your parents got divorced when you were a little boy. Did you cry when your parents told you? Did you ever do things that you knew were wrong because you were mad about your dad leaving?

3. Are there any foods you can't eat? My mom can't eat gluten because she has celiac disease. Can you make a law so that there are more gluten-free foods for people with celiac disease to eat?

4. Do your kids ever bother you when you are working and do you send them to timeout?

5. Can you make a law so that prices in grocery stores are cheaper?

6. Do you ever feel like you have too much work being in charge of the world?

7. Did you like to talk a lot when you were a kid? I love to talk.

I know you will make the earth a better place to live. I hope you have a great time being the President. Write back soon!

From,
Julia, age 7
Gaithersburg, MD

Dear President Obama,

How are you doing Mr. President? Are you a nice person? When I hear you speak, I think you sound like a nice person. Do you help your wife with any chores? My dad helps sweep the floors and take out the trash. Will your kids have chores in the White house? I have to feed my dog, gather laundry, and keep my room clean. What is your favorite book? Mine is any book in the series, *Hank the Cowdog.* I would suggest you introduce your girls to these books if they do not already know about them. Do you like snakes? I think snakes are gorgeous. I would love to see the White House. Could you tell me what it is like inside and out?

> Sincerely,
> Jeremiah, age 11
> Knox City, TX

Dear President Obama,

I have a few questions for you.

1. Can you lower college prices? I think they are way too expensive. I care because I am going to college and I don't want to be poor.
2. Can you lower gas prices to 1 cent? If we all have to pay $50 to get gas, we will end up not having any money for food and water. I care because when I grow up, I might have to handle this situation.

My three-year old sister wants me to ask you if you know about Pokemon. Even though I like Pokemon, I kind of think it's a dumb question.

Gavin, age 8
Chicago, IL

Dear President Obama,

If I were president, I would say no more littering. I would put up signs. I would make it a law. I would make it a policy. I would put up posters. I would send police to whoever litters and say to that person not to litter again.

Let me ask you some questions. What sport do you like? What is your favorite color? What is your favorite amusement park? Who is your favorite author? What is your favorite holiday? What is your favorite hobby? What is your favorite season? What is your favorite movie? What is your favorite plant? What is your favorite planet? Who is your favorite scientist? Who is your favorite artist? What is your favorite candy? What is your favorite state? Who is your favorite illustrator? What is your favorite store? What is your favorite restaurant? What is your favorite computer? What is your favorite animal? That's all the questions I need to ask you.

Best wishes,

Alex, age 8
Sherman Oaks, CA

Dear President Obama,

I have always wondered what it is like to be president like you. I think it would be dreadfully busy, going to meetings, signing papers, going to other countries to meet their leaders and stuff like that. Do you get any time with your kids? It is hard to believe that you'd get any time with them, with all that work and all the meetings.

Is there anything made out of pure gold in the White House? If so, make sure nothing like that tips on you, your wife, or the first dog. That would really hurt!

From,
Richard, age 10
Kensington, MD

Dear President Obama,

Do you think you'll mind having bigger responsibilities than you did in the Senate? Do you think that your family will like living in the White House? I think it would be really nice to live in the White House, but it would get really annoying with all the reporters following me around like a dog. How do you feel about being the president of the United States? Does some of your inspiration come from Abraham Lincoln?

I'm really glad that you became president.

Sincerely,
Catherine, age 10
Houston, TX

Dear President Obama,

I think you should help all the poar people get food, and water and money. Do you like being the president? I want to know if you like the Cubs Or the White sox? Do you get breakfast in bed? Should all of America stop littering? The playgrund neads a new seasow. What is the new dog's name? Do you know if the dog is haveing pupys yet?

Your Friend,
Ben

Ben, age 6½
Evanston, IL

Ben, age 6½

Evanston, IL

Dear President Obama,

I was wondering if you get to keep your personal Blackberry phone. I do not understand why you might not be able to keep your personal phone. All of your friends and family already have that number.

I also would like to talk about how the Whitehouse looks. I have never been there. I might not ever get to go either since it is so far away. What is it like on the inside and outside? How many rooms do you have? Does the grass there stay green year around? I suppose you have some plants and flowers outside too. Can your girls pick flowers at the Whitehouse? I guess your floors inside the Whitehouse stay shiny all the time. Do your walls stay clean and shiny also? Are there people in the Whitehouse that keep it clean and pretty or do you have to do it also? What was your first reaction when you stepped into the Whitehouse knowing it was your new home? Were your two daughters and wife happy also?

I hope you enjoyed my letter. I also hope I get some answers!

Love,
Jessica, age 9
Knox City, TX

P.S. I hope your family is happy living in the Whitehouse. I wish you well for the next four years.

Dear President Obama,

Oh, what a handful of questions I have! But I'll only ask you a few. I would first like to know, when did you decide to become president? I mean, did you say you wanted to become president in law school, college, high school, junior high, elementary, or maybe as young as kindergarten (and no one believed you)? If you had said so at that age, I bet your kindergarten teacher cried when you got nominated. Next, when people dropped out of the primary elections, did you feel triumph or sorrow? Lastly, do you feel the legislative branch is with you or against you?

I have especially chosen these questions because I hope you feel good, not bad. I am very happy for you. I understand it is very overwhelming, running America. . . .

Sincerely,
Camilo, age 10
Tacoma Park, MD

Dear President Obama,

Why don't you make more schools? Why don't you give people money because they work so hard, they deserve it. Why don't you make kids happy? To make people happy, make them spend time together.

From your pal,
Alisa, age 6
Evanston, IL

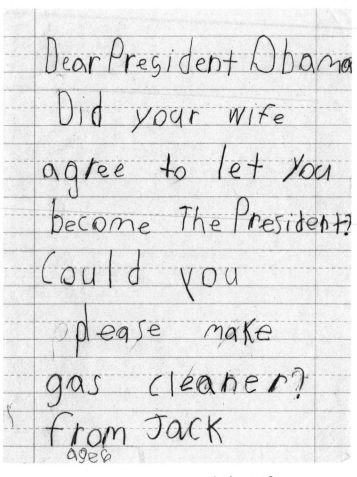

Dear President Obama
Did your wife
agree to let you
become The President?
Could you
please make
gas cleaner?
from Jack
age 6

Jack, age 6
East Northport, N.Y.

Dear President Obama,

I wanted to tell you that I am glad that you were elected our President. I have some questions that I would like to ask you, as follows: Can you help the homeless kids to get some homes? Can you make the orphanages more comfortable and cozy for the kids?

I also wanted to ask you why everything that we have to buy is so expensive? Why did they stop building houses everywhere? Why are the stores closing? Why are the car dealerships closing? I really like new cars and I like to look at them, but a lot of the places that sell them have closed. Why is gas going down? I think that is a good thing that the price of gas is going down.

What are your plans as our President? What do you do as President? Do you have a regular family? Do your daughters go to a regular school? Does your wife have a job? Did you get a dog? Do you think that things in our country will be better when you are President? I hope that you can answer some of my questions.

Sincerely,
Kali, age 8
Sumner, WA

Dear President Obama,

Do you think being president is hard? Do you like being President? What is your favorite color? What is your favorite food? Do you like sports? What is your favorite sport? What is your favorite season? Do you have any trophies? Do you like the White House? Do you have morning calls? What is your favorite drink? What is your favorite movie? What is your favorite picture? Do you like playing cards? Do you have decorations in your room? What is your favorite TV show? Do you have an iPod? Have you ever made sand art? What is your favorite animal?

I want a world of peace. I want recess before lunch because if we didn't have recess before lunch we would get cramps.

I wish there could be more indoor water parks. I wish there could be more baseball games and football games. I wish there could be more board games. I wish they could stop cutting down trees. I wish there could be more companies because my uncle lost his job and I wish he could get a new one.

Good luck!
Jacob, age 7
Simsbury, CT

Dear President Obama,

I am your biggest fan in the whole world. I was the happiest kid in the whole universe when you were announced president.

When you got into Harvard Law School were you really excited? How long did it take to become a lawyer, then into a senator, and then a president? My sister is going to be a lawyer. Do you have any advice for her?

Please help the US as much as you can! Do your best as president of the U.S.A.

Sincerely,
Enriques, age 10
Silver Spring, MD

Dear President Obama,

I'm your biggest fan and I have 5 questions. Here they are.

1. Can you help us with the war?
2. Are you good at running the country?
3. Do you know how to bake cookies?
4. My dad trades shares and I wanted to know if you could lower some. Well, I don't know but I think they're called shares.
5. Can you come to our class one day?
6. Can you read Torah?

Sincerely,
Your biggest fan,
Zack, age 9
Rochester, N.Y.

Dear Obama,

How do you handle all these bad comments that people make about you? I couldn't stand it if someone treated me like that.

> From,
> Marc, age 12
> Doylestown, PA

Dear President Obama,

I'm so glad you became our president. Will you get to pick out a brand new car? If I were president, I would pick a black convertible. I was wondering when your birthday is. Mine is on March 27th. Has your family adjusted well in the White House? If I ever lived there, it might take me a while to get used to it. My last question is how hard is it to be the president? I think it would be real hard to not make people mad.

> Your Friend,
> Avery, age 10
> Knox City, TX

Dear President Obama,

How does it feel to be president? My sister wants to know that. She is three and a half. And also, how does it feel to be in the White House?

Are you going to get a pet? I think you should get a

dog and a hamster for the girls. What are you gonna like mostest about being president? Why did you want to be president?

Be a very good president, okay? I hope that you are gonna make good decisions. I want you to care about schools. I am in kindergarten.

I am so happy that you are president!

> Sophia, age 5
> Takoma Park, MD

Dear President Obama,

How old are you? I am eight. What do you do on Friday nights? Do you have any pets? I do, I have 2 dogs and 5 fish and 6 cats. They are nice. Do you write a lot? I do in school. What school did you go to when you were a little kid?

I hope you have fun at the White House.

> Sincerely,
> Michaela, age 8
> Hoosick Falls, N.Y.

Dear President Obama,
Your girls are pretty. Did You
buy your girls a puppy?
Who cleans up the white House?
What Sheets does your girls
have on ther beds?
What does it feel like being
President?
I like puppys too!
                              Love,
                         ANAmaria

Ana (Anamaria), age 6
Skokie, IL

Dear President Obama,

If I was old enough to vote, I would have voted for you. Luckily, I did get to vote for you using "Nickelodeon Kids Pick the President" online.

I hope you can figure out a way to stop global warming, because I don't want the polar bears and penguins to go extinct. I also don't want the trees to all die off, as well as the rain forests.

I also hope you can stop the bank problems as well as the stock market crashes. Lots of people are having huge money problems, and my family is having small money problems, as well. I would also like you to stop the stock market problems.

I REALLY hope you can stop all the wars going on or this could become World War III.

I also have a few questions for you:

1. Do you think it's fun being President of the United States?
2. Do you think it's fair that quite a lot of people have a bigger salary than the President of the United States?
3. What school did you go to?
4. What kind of sports did you play?
5. What breed of puppy are you getting for your daughters?

Sincerely,
Andy, age 12
West Linn, OR

CHAPTER 4

Now Let Me Tell You a Bit About Myself

It's amazing how comfortable kids seem to feel writing to the president. They introduce themselves and tell him all kinds of things about their lives. They invite him over, they give him their phone numbers, and they feel confident that he's interested in where they go to school and what sports they play and what they think about the world.

They're probably right. What matters most to children—family, schooling, feeling hopeful about the future, feeling secure in the world, and helping those in need—were the themes of Barack Obama's campaign, themes he echoed in his inaugural address.

If his young correspondents could only meet him and tell him face-to-face what they've written here about their lives, he probably would be every bit as interested as they're hoping he'd be. But maybe that's not so surprising, as these kids have been up to quite a lot!

Dear President Obama:

I feel like I'm a lot like you, even down to pretty small details. The thing that is most similar, I think, is that I barely know my father. He came from Cameroon, Africa to study at Howard University in Washington, D.C. He stayed in America for awhile, where he met my mother who is white. He went back to Cameroon when I was really little and I haven't seen him since I was a few months old. I've seen pictures of him and heard lots of stories about him from my mom and my uncle. I've always hoped he would come back. I guess God gave me my wish, because my dad is coming to visit me in March!

Since I'm around the same age you were when your father visited you, I want to ask what that felt like for you. I am feeling scared, worried, confident, happy, excited and all of them at the same time. I also have fears that my father won't like me. Were you scared about that too? Did your father like you when he met you? I hope it's okay for me to ask you about this because I really need some advice.

When I hear you speak I believe in you and then I reflect on our similarities and I believe in myself, too!

Thank you for reading my letter.

Sincerely,
Malik, age 12
Silver Spring, MD

Dear President Obama,

Let me tell you about me. I like to draw and read. I am 7 years old. I live in Sherman Oaks. My mom was born in Norway and my dad was born in India. That's all about me.

If I were president I would help other people. I would help people by giving some money to them. I would also give some food. I would give toys. That's what I would do.

Sincerely,
Hans, age 7
Sherman Oaks, CA

Dear President Obama,

My name is Victoria Isabella. I am six years old. I am very happy that you are the President because you are good man.

I wrote a mini-poem for you:

President Obama has a big heart.
He is the best of the best
Because he is very kind and smart
And he always passes all his tests.

I live with my parents in Virginia. I have two sets of grandparents. I have many friends. Some of my good friends are Republican but that is O.K. I am also a flamenco dancer. I hope you will invite me to make a flamenco presentation in the White House. You will like it.

I also want to invite you to visit Venezuela. Two of my grandparents are from Venezuela. My great-grandmother has a big house in a city called Valle de la Pascua. Your wife and your daughters can come with you and stay with my great-grandmother. She will cook good Venezuelan food for you and your family. The food will make you smarter and a greater president. You will become EL PRESIDENTE MAS GRANDE.

I wish you a very good Christmas. Please ask Santa Claus for plane tickets to Venezuela so you and your family can travel to Venezuela next year.

> Buena suerte!
> Victoria Isabella, age 6
> Manassas, VA

Dear President Obama,

I saw you in Seattle one year ago, and since then I have been very busy (but I expect you've been busier than me). I have started a Government class and I like it very much. In it we learn about the election process and the past presidents. I love politics and when I was seven I could name every president and vice president America has ever had! In my class I am running for president against two other groups (each group has a presidential and vice-presidential candidate, an artistic supervisor and campaign manager). We need to write a speech to explain what we are running for. My vice-presidential candidate and I have already written our speeches. Everyone in class is homeschooled. I also take taekwondo lessons, band, and I'm learning from my mom and grandma to play piano.

Nicholas, age 11
Covington, WA

Dear President Obama,

How's it going? I'm doing great. Really quick, I'll tell you some things about myself. I'm a six foot four thirteen-year-old. I'm in the eighth grade, I play bass in our school orchestra, I read and write a lot, and I'm not a bad artist.

Whenever you get to go to the library, ask for the book, *The House on Mango Street,* by Sandra Cisneros. It's a really good book.

Thank you for reading my letter to you.

With best wishes,
Freddy, age 13
Fort Worth, TX

Dear President Obama,

My name is Cory and I have done Meals On Wheels deliveries for seven years. Every week my grandpa and I deliver meals to the needy. I am ten years old and I started when I was three. The reason I like delivering meals is because I am giving, not getting. This month I am collecting food to donate to Meals On Wheels. My goal is to make sure no one is hungry this Thanksgiving.

I understand that you are a big fan of community service too. I think that it is great that you are giving college assistance to people who do community service. I can't wait to take advantage of this program when I'm ready for college.

Thank you for taking the time to read this. Good luck as President.

Sincerely,
Cory, age 10
Greenville, S.C.

Dear President Obama:

You are my hero! Now I know that I can be anything that I put my mind to! My name is Maaseiah. I am 7 years old like your daughter Sasha. I am a second grade student in Atlanta, Georgia. I am smart and I'm a genius. I mean triple smart and a genius. Guess what I want to be when I grow up? I want to be a doctor so I can heal people all over the world. I want to help the unfortunate poor people in America and in developing countries like your father's native country, Kenya. However, as a future doctor, I am concerned that I won't be able to help all of my patients due to all of the issues with our current health care system.

As you move into the White House with your own young children, remember that all of America's children need a strong champion. You and your new administration can fulfill that role by standing up for kids across America.

Your greatest fan,
Maaseiah, age 7
Atlanta, GA

メリーマウント英語学校

オバマさん　おめでとう

　　　　私の名前は、多賀牧穂です。日本から
来ました。今は10さいでローマに住んでいます。私はメリーマウント
英語学校にかよっています。私たちはが死について学んでいます。
あなたはしっていますか。923万人の人々がベッドでおなかがすいて
ねむれないこと。だから、たすけましょうと言うことで、学校では、
が死をなくすためのくふうをしています。
　　　新しい しごと がんばってください。
　　　　　　　　　　　　　　　　　まきほ

Makiho, age 10
Rome, Italy

This is the translation of Makiho's letter.

Dear President Obama,

My name is Makiho. I come from Japan. I am 10 years old and I live in Rome. I go to Marymount International School. In ESL [English as a second language] we are learning about hunger in our world. Did you know 923 million people go to bed hungry? Did you know also over half the world's population live in Asia and the Pacific and nearly two thirds of the world's hungry people live there? They need help. So we asked all the teachers and students in our school to give us ideas for stopping hunger. Can you help? Congratulations on your new job.

From,
Makiho, age 10
Rome, Italy

Dear President Obama,

I am from Israel. Some people in Israel think that you will make Israel an Arab country, but I beg to differ. I think you will make Israel a better place. I like America a lot and I visit there a lot, and I hope you do good to America. By the way, I want to ask you about your childhood. Where did you grow up and what was your favorite sport? And when you were growing up, did you think of being president?

From,
Yair, age 9
Jerusalem, Israel

Dear President Obama,

My name is Safia and I am 7 years old. I was born in Cedars Sinai Hospital. For Thanksgiving I had turkey, cranberry sauce, bread and coligreens. I have over one hundred books at home. My favorite animal is a dolphin and a penguin. My favorite toy is a slinky. My family is from Atlanta. I am from California.

Why do you want to be president? You are going to be the best president ever!

Your fan,
Safia, age 7
Sherman Oaks, CA

Dear President Obama,

My name is Melando. I want to ask you some questions. What was it like when you were a child? Was your TV black and white? Did you have toys? Did you ever play any instruments? I play the piano. Why did you want to be President? What is it like to be President? Is it a lot of work? What good things will you do for our country? One day I will be a good President like you.

By the way, I am 7 years old. I like to play sports like football, soccer, baseball and basketball. Football is my favorite sport. I played for the Chargers this year and we finished in first place. It was a fun season. I also have fun playing my Xbox 360. My favorite game is Lego Star Wars. I am in the 2nd grade at a good school. I have learned a lot so far this year. Did you enjoy school when you were growing up? I enjoy it and try to make my parents proud of me. My parents are cool.

I am glad that you won the election. I know that you have a tough job ahead of you. I wish the best of luck to you, President Obama, in the future. I hope that you can make our country a better place to live.

Sincerely,
Melando, age 7
Virginia Beach, VA

Dear President Obama,

My family went to Disneyland this summer when gas prices were extremely high. We had to hold up on some fun things so that we could have money to drive. I carpool every day to school even though gas prices are going down. What are you going to do about the problem of pollution and gas prices?

I hope you make great changes for the future. I hope your family is happy and healthy.

Sincerely,
Farrell, age 11
South Weber, UT

Dear President Obama,

I heard that you relied on your mom and grandmother. My parents have been divorced for about a year now and it's really hard to handle. I depend on my great aunt a lot, because my mom works early in the morning to nighttime, six days a week. I'm just wondering how you dealt with this in your childhood.

Sincerely,
Crystal, age 14
Fort Worth, TX

Dear President Obama,

When I was four year old I became a citizen of the United States of America. It meant a lot to me. I was no longer an alien, no longer that much different. I hope the United States will help keep the earth go round.

I think it would be a good idea to have more solar powered houses and cars, and wind powered electricity. Make more energy efficient cars and less gas guzzling airplanes, because I want there to be more ice in the polar regions so that animals can keep living there. I really like penguins, and they need ice. I take photos, and I love taking ones of birds and their spirits.

Meiling, age 12
Des Moines, WA

Dear President Obama,

My first name is Delaney and my middle name is Kimiko. I am 7 years old and am a first grader. At my school we learn about other cultures, especially Japan. We spend half of our day at school speaking and writing Japanese. It's interesting and important because if we understand each other we will not have war. If we understand each other then we won't hurt each other.

At my school, if two kids are fighting, we have to make choices to stop fighting, talk it out, get help, or walk away. War is a bad answer for problems.

Thank you, Mr. President Obama. I'm glad you are president. Say hi to Hillary Clinton for me and your daughters, especially your 7 year old. Maybe we could be friends!

Sincerely,
Delaney, age 7
Portland, OR

Dear President Obama,

I am a ten year old, middle class girl who usually is not too interested in the elections, but this year has been different. My family and I watched the majority of your debates during dinner in our shingled home in Berkeley, California. We agreed that you appeared totally composed. I am a mixture of Jewish, American, and Pakistani descent. My father is a Muslim by birth and my mother converted to Islam so my siblings and I were born Muslim.

We are very excited about your election because it's also creating a chance for many people of all backgrounds and ethnicities to become President. People who never bothered to vote have voted in this election. The

American people need a good leader who can help them out of these economic bad times.

I wish you a successful term.

Sincerely,
Zohra, age 10
Berkeley, CA

Dear President Obama

I saw you on the television and I like it when you talk to us and tell us about the world. When you come to Seattle, I would like to meet you and play piano for you. I can also dance ballet really good.

Victoria, age 6
Bothell, WA

Dear President Obama,

You are a huge role-model in my life. You have influenced me to be humble, strong, a great leader, and to make history. I would like to be President of the United States, too. I'll tell you a little bit about myself. One thing that we have in common is that our names are unique. My first name, Hasani, means handsome in Northern Arabic and my middle name, Akil, means intelligent one in Swahili. My last name originated from my father's Jamaican ancestors. Similar to you, my parents are from two different countries, my mother is American and my father is Jamaican. I'm eleven years old and in the sixth grade.

President Obama, I understand that you are a very important person, but I was wondering if sometime maybe you would consider stopping by Grand Rapids to meet my family and my class. You can reach me at (616) XXX-XXXX. Thank you for your time and I am positive that you will be the best President America has had!

Your new friend,
Hasani, age 11
Grand Rapids, MI

Dear Mr. Obama,

My name is Ethan. I am 11 years old and I'm in 6th grade. I live with my 2 older sisters and 1 younger brother, also my mom and dad. I am a 2nd generation Vietnamese/American. My parents were from Vietnam. I speak both Vietnamese and English fluently (Vietnamese less than English).

I am really glad that you are my president and I trust that you will keep me and the rest of the people of the United States safe and happy. I am wondering, though, what would you do if another country attacks us? I know that you will find a way to fix it, I'm sure of it. I know you will be a great president because you know what this country needs and you know how to achieve it. Thank you, Mr. Obama, for reading my letter. Please write back.

Sincerely,
Ethan, age 11
West Linn, OR

Dear President Obama,
My name is Vanessa.

I magine you were a child again and your parents were going to get a divorce. What would you do?

What do you do in the White house? My favorite color is red and I got red highlights in my hair. I have a brother but he is at my dad's. I am asking you what would you do if your parents gat Divorced becaues my parents are gatting divorced. But I think it will be the best for them. Because if they didn't I would hear them fight all day and nigth

Thank you for reading my letter
your
friend,
Vanessa

Vanessa, age 10
Des Moines, IA

Dear Mr. President Obama,

I am so excited to be writing to you, I can hardly sit still!!! (My mom is typing this letter because she types faster and neater than I write. But I am working on my writing, even though it hurts my hand to write too much. My mom says that is no excuse and I still have to try.) I hope you really do read my letter.

I like to travel to different places just like you. So far I have only been to Wisconsin Dells. But my parents say we may go to Niagara Falls this summer or Florida's seaside. Have you ever been to either of these two places? Next, next summer, we may even go to China with my Grandma! My Grandma says I have to be able to sit still for a long time because the airplane ride is like 8900 hours long!! My dad says that they have the best food markets there. Have you ever been to China to try the food markets? What has been your favorite place to visit?

I was wondering, what was your favorite subject in school? Mine is "free time", though my mom says that is not a subject in school. I like free time because I get to play robots, and Star Wars with my friends. If we got graded for free time I am sure I would get an A+! Do you get much free time? (My mom says no, but you have to, right? You are the President, you get to do whatever you want.) If I was President I would make the school give grades for free time.

I know you will be a great leader and help out all the people who have no homes, jobs, and money. You promised, remember? And adults should always try hard to keep their promise, like my parents. My parents says you will, and I believe them because they are smart people.

I hope you enjoyed my letter and will write back because that will be so cool. I can show all my friends and they'd think I rock!

> Thank you,
> Rex, age 7
> Chicago, IL

Dear Mr. President,

I'm ten years old and I live in California and I play basketball and I am a green and black stripe in Tae Kwon Do.

Did you know that you changed history by being the 1st African-American president? I am happy to have seen history change. Do you like being president? Why did you pick Senator Biden for vice president? Is being president hard work?

I felt like I needed to ask these questions because I've never written a letter to a president before. I have a dream of being a president when I'm older too, or I might be a professional basketball player. Anyways, I hope you like the job.

> Sincerely,
> Arielle, age 10
> Toluca Lake, CA

Dear President Obama,

You inspire me and all my friends. I think you will do a good job. I feel a special connection to you because like you I have a mixed background. My father is white American and my mother is from India. Like you, I have relatives that come from different countries including America, India, El Salvador, and Denmark. I am excited because you are a truly "American" president of America's melting pot.

Right now I am living in Mumbai, India for a year with my parents. Things are really tense here after the terrorist attacks. I feel sad and angry. I am sad for all the people that were killed. I am angry that the terrorists caused so much destruction. I feel lucky to be safe because we have been to the Taj hotel for high tea, and to the Gateway of India many times.

If the U.S. wants to do something about the India-Pakistan relationship, it should be the peacemaker and be neutral with both countries. Since I am living here now, I hope you can do that. I would like America to help make the world more peaceful and stop wars. I think we can also help with sports, better libraries and good computers for school children. Can we? Yes we can!!!!!!

I look forward to you having you as President. Good luck.

Peace,
Arjun, age 10
Mumbai, India

Dear President Obama,

    I'm going to tell you about my life. I love dragons. I like dinosaurs. I'm seven years old. I'm going to be a business mogle when I grow up. I like cars. My favorite month is December. My birthday is on December twenty second. That's every thing about me.

    I'm going to ask you questions now. Why do you want to be president? Where are you from? How old are you? Do you have any friends? That's all of my questions.

                Best Wishes,
                Orion

Orion, age 8
Studio City, CA

Dear President Obama,

My mom is the greatest mom. She bought me a puppy and we named him Fred. She keeps me safe and she loves me like your mom loved you. My aunt and uncle went to heaven this year and it was very sad. I know how sad you must be losing your nanny [grandmother] and your mom. Mommy says every year good things and bad things happen. She says we should remember the good and throw away the bad.

> From
> Nick, age 9
> Northport, N.Y.

Dear President Obama,

I'm glad we have a man like you as president. My step-dad is an immigrant and he has been living here for many years and working hard. I think that if you do something about the problems of immigrants, you will have many hard workers. Many people come to America to have a better life, because over there in Mexico, we don't have many jobs and opportunities like we have here.

Thank you for doing something about education, too.
You rock, Mr. President Obama!!

> Sincerely,
> Tania, age 14
> Fort Worth, TX

Dear President Obama,

My name is Hanna. Currently, I am 10 years old. I am the rare daughter in a large family with five brothers, nine cats, two dogs, and approximately eighty chickens! My mother is a teacher in a Muslim homeschooling cooperative with intelligent pupils representing nineteen different nationalities. My father is a real estate developer in San Francisco. I am of Korean and American descent. I am a practicing Muslim, and I LOVE to eat; but fortunately I am not stout! I also enjoy horseback riding, reading, writing, and bossing little brothers around.

As I mentioned, I am a practicing Muslim and my religion is very important to me. I know your father was a Muslim. You must know and, as president, help others to understand that we are loving, generous, and peaceful people.

I also NEED my dad to keep his job which means you will have to restore the economy. My family owns a 22 acre ranch which is very meaningful to me and my kin. I love to be there in the early morning feeling the gentle wind blowing on my cheeks and watching the animals munch hungrily on their breakfast. The ranch is an essential component of my childhood, and if you don't fix the economy, we might lose it.

As you see, my family, religion, and ranch are significant aspects in the life of this 10 year old California girl. I believe in you, President Obama, and your ability and desire to make this country a better place.

Sincerely,
Hanna, age 10
Lafayette, CA

P.S. Would you mind sending me a chocolate cake and some coffee flavored ice cream? Yum. Yum. (And I'm very serious.)

Dear President Obama,

I'm going to tell you about myself, President Obama. My favorite foods are macaroni, pizza, spaghetti, and pasta. My sister is five months old. My family is nice and courteous. I have a beautiful life.

If I were president, I would answer any question in the world. So I could have good ideas, by thinking of all the answers. I could brainstorm so I can get all the answers. When people ask me questions, I would answer them. I'm going to have fun answering those questions.

> Love,
> David, age 7
> Los Angeles, CA

Dear President Obama,

My name is Renée and I am 7 years old. I live in Markham, Canada. I like your family name, Obama. How is your family? Did you have a good time in your old job? What movies do you like? I enjoyed *Mamma Mia.* Where have you traveled? I have traveled to many places myself: Cuba, Trinidad & Tobago, Dominican Republic, Japan, and Guam. I liked Cuba best. Would you like to visit us in Canada? What do you like to eat? My favorite foods to eat are noodles, rice, salad, bread, vegetables, especially broccoli, beef, chicken, seafood, and most appetizers, and chow mein.

Do you have to water your gardens in the White House? I saw your house in November when I went to my cousin's wedding and there is a lot of grass to water.

Hope you have fun in your new job.

Love
Renée, age 7
Markham, Canada

Dear President Obama,

I like America because I love good stories and American libraries. I came from Iran three years ago. Why do small toys cost so much money? It is not right.

Sincerely,
Adrian, age 7
Glendale, CA

Dear President Obama,

My name is Emma. I am 7 and three quarters. My skin color is light brown. My hair color is dark brown. My heritage is Korean and Filipino. When I grow up I want to be president like you.

What college did you go to? Well, I might go to Harvard or the one you went to and maybe Stanford. My friend's sister went to Stanford. I am thinking of advanced schools when I get older. Especially college because I want to be a president just like you. I hope I do because I get 4s and 3s for my grades.

Your citizen,
Emma, age 7³/₄
Sherman Oaks, CA

This letter was dictated by a 5-year-old to his mother. He is of Caribbean/Danish heritage and is the only biracial boy in his kindergarten class in Copenhagen. His mother reports: "When he first saw Obama on TV and in the newspapers, he said, 'Mommy, Mommy, he is brown like me.' I know the kindergarten children followed the election, since Ajani would come home singing, 'Obama, Obama, O yeah!' "

Dear President Obama,

I am a little brown boy like you and I live with my Mommy and Daddy and my Cousin Idlyn. I know that you live in The News and that you are The Good One.

I like being silly and playing computer games, watching *Kung Fu Panda* and karate—"Haaa! Yaaa! Kachuuuu!" My favorite food is soup with dumplings and sweet dessert. Do you know what dumplings are? You make them with flour and water and mix them in a bowl and roll them in your hands like so and put them in the soup. They are delicious. I can speak English and Danish and sometimes Kweyol; not all the time. But my mommy can speak Kweyol all the time.

I don't know what a President does but I know that

being a President is hard; it is not easy, not easy, not easy. As president you should do good things, not bad things. You should be friends with everyone and John McCain. And when the people are sad you should pat them on the back so they can be glad.

I wish everyone in the world, our Earth, to be friends and to share their toys and play together.

Sincerely,
Ajani, age 5
Copenhagen, Denmark

CHAPTER 5

Say Hi to Your Daughters for Me—and Mrs. Obama and Your Dog

★

The eleven-and-unders were especially excited to have a First Family that included young children like them, and that came through unmistakably in their letters. Kids had lots of questions for Malia and Sasha, and even a few for the First Lady. They wondered what it's like to live in the White House, or even imagined what it must be like to have all that room to run around. Of course, quite a few offered to come over for a playdate with the girls.

What really caught kids' interest and brought forth their expertise was the question of pet ownership. Kids who have a dog were quick to recommend their specific breed. Like all good, persuasive writers, they used examples based on their own experience, and argued their cases with both passion and evidence. It's a shame that the First Family can't have one of each breed recommended in these letters.

Dear President Obama,

Do your girls get everything they want now that you are the President? You have all the money in the world now. Could they paint their room pink if they wanted it that color? Do they have their own bathroom? They are so lucky to live in the best house in the world!

I am so excited that I had the chance to write you a letter.

Love,
Tiffany, age 10
Knox City, TX

Dear President Obama,

Can I come for a sleepover with Sasha at the White House? I've never been to a sleepover before and that would be super fun!

Your Friend,
Eliana, age 6
Salem, OR

Leilani, age 6
Evanston, IL

Dear President Obama,

Do you have the dog like you promised Malia and Sasha? What kind of bed do they have? I am sure that they are going to like it. Do you really like chili? I love chili.

> By your pal,
> Leilani, age 6
> Evanston, IL

Dear President Obama,

I have a dog by the name of Cody. He is a Border Collie who can play soccer. If you have not made a choice in the type of dog you will be getting, I highly suggest getting a Border Collie because they are children lovers and highly active. If you do not like Border Collies for whatever reason, I have two more types that would be good for your family, especially your girls! The first breed is a Collie. They are a very loyal and trusting breed. The next breed you might consider is the Labrador. This breed is the #1 dog of America. If you do not like any of these choices, I am sure any dog will do in the White House.

I would like to be an animal in the White House! I can just imagine what I would see and hear. I was also wondering one more thing. How old are your girls? I am nine, almost ten. Would they like a pen pal? I am not even sure if kids who live in the White House can have pen pals.

I am sure you are a busy man, so I had better let you go!

Your Animal Lover,
Katelynn, age 9
Knox City, TX

P.S. Do you think you could have soccer-playing dogs in the White House?

Dear President Obama,

I have a question for Malia. What's your favorite thing to watch on television? When you get older, what would you like to be when you grow up? This question is for Sasha: When you grow up what would you like to be?

Michelle Obama, when you're not on the road or with Mr. Obama, what do you like to do in your spare time?

I have something else I would like to say, also: I love the way you do things because when you do it, you look so laid back and cool. When you walk and talk, you look and sound like a nice and clean president. You also seem like a responsible gentlemen. You are my favorite and most honorable person ever. You are my best role model and I have a tremendous amount of respect for you. I glad you are president because you are an intelligent man and you have a lot of honor and respect inside of you with a big heart.

Sincerely,
Ja'Quan, age 10
Newport News, VA

P.S. Tell Michelle Obama, Malia Obama, and Sasha Obama I said have a nice and good life and for you, Mr. Obama, I hope you have a good time in the White House and become a good president. I have one more question, if you like football who's your favorite football team? Well, if you see this letter I hope you like it and I would like you to try to write back soon!!!!!

Dear President Obama,

We are very excited that you have two girls who are almost the same age as us. We have a new puppy, Roxie, who is a Havanese. She doesn't shed and is good if you are allergic. We would like to have a playdate with Malia and Sasha after they get their puppy, and then our puppies can play together too.

> Sincerely,
> Chloe, age 8, and
> Sasha, age 6
> New York, N.Y.

Dear Mr. Obama:

I have a couple of questions for your daughters. One is, What is it like having the President of the United States for a dad? Also, what's it like to live in the White House?

Thanks for your time.

Sincerely,
Gunnar, age 11
West Linn, OR

Dear President Obama,

I heard you are looking for a dog. I think you should get a pit bull because they are cool. They are good at chase and hide-and-seek. However they are a loud breed that is annoying. Your girls will like it. I have one myself. It's name is Hensm. Don't keep them outside if it is thundering.

Sincerely,
Devin, age 10
Heber Springs, AR

Dear President Obama,

Do you think you will have time to read to your daughters?

Your American Citizen,
Ryan, age 8
Hoosick Falls, N.Y.

Dear President OBama,
I wish you wehe IN ThIS
CLASS. Do Your JiRIS heve
HaNNa MONTaNa and TiNKeh
Bell? NATHAN

Nathan, age 6
Chicago, IL

Dear Mr. Obama,

What will you do for fun with your daughters each week? Pizza night? Movie night?

I am hoping things will get better during your presidency, Mr. Obama. I watch the news with my parents at dinner and my parents make noises when the economy is mentioned by Charlie Gibson.

Well, anyway, good luck. I hope to meet you someday to say Hello!

> Lily, age 8
> Califon, N.J.

Dear President Barack Obama,

My name is Monica and I love to sing. Please tell our First Lady Michelle, Sasha and Malia that I said hi. I am enormously joyful that you are president of the United States of America. I would like to sing for you.

> Sincerely,
> Monica, age 13
> Philadelphia, PA

Dear President Obama,

I heard that you promised Malia and Sasha a puppy. I know a good breed. I would suggest a teacup Chihuahua.

It wouldn't take up a lot of space, it only gets to be the size of a teacup. They are playful, kind, and not that loud. They are very good hiders, so I recommend you keep your house clean, so it doesn't get lost. I hope you find a dog.

> Sincerely,
> Lauren, age 8
> Heber Springs, AR

Dear President Obama,

I know you are a very busy man being the president and you fly all over the world and things like that, but do you get leisure time to spend with your family that supports you 100% of the time? Was it hard for Sasha and Malia to leave all of their friends in Chicago? What do you miss most about living in Chicago?

I am glad that you have become our brand new president of the United States of America.

We are depending on you, President Obama,

> Yelena, age 11
> Doylestown, PA

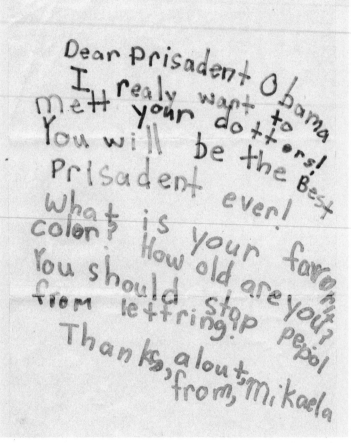

Dear Prisadent Obama
I realy want to mett your dottors!
You will be the Best Prisadent ever!
What is your favorit color?
How old are you?
You should stop peppol from lettring.
Thanks, a lout, from, Mikaela

Mikaela, age 7
Takoma Park, MD

Dear President Obama,

We think it will be really nice for your family to live in the White House. Always keep your piano tuned! When we went through the White House on a tour, we saw a piano-tuner tuning the piano, and we think it is very important to keep an instrument in tune if Sasha or Malia wants to play piano. If they play piano, they should have one break day, and the rest of the days for practicing, except if they have an activity like soccer; those days are *off.* But also we think that the lesson counts as a practice time.

> Sincerely,
> Hilda, age 7,
> and Carmen, age 5
> Chevy Chase, MD

Dear President Obama,

One day I would like to come to the White House and meet you and your family, would that be possible? Can I become a pen pal with one or both of your daughters? Do your daughters get to have a regular kid life? Is it possible that kids could come to the White House to have a play date with your girls'?

> Sincerely,
> Aliyah, age 11
> Sumner, WA

Dear Presidet- Elect Obama,

I new you are looking for a dog to take whith you to the Wite Houes. I think you should get a pug becose they like to run and your douters could run with the dog to get excersiz. I hope you like your new dog.

Sincerely,
Haydan

Haydan, age 8
Tumbling Shoals, AR

Dear President Obama,

My Dad went to college with Ms. Michelle and I think Ms. Michelle is very nice and will make a great First Lady. I hope you and your family have a good time in the White House. I am very excited that you are President of the United States because I am an African-American and you look like me! I really like you because you lived in Hawaii and Shane Victorino, of the Philadelphia Phillies, is my favorite baseball player and he is from Hawaii also. I just want to say that you being the first African-American president means that I am really special. I hope you will change the world so that there is less violence.

> Love,
> Duarte, age 7
> Philadelphia, PA

Dear Mr. President:

I heard that you are getting a puppy for your two daughters. I was glad to hear that you're thinking of adopting from the pound rather than buying a purebred dog, when there are plenty of dogs looking for homes and people to take care of them.

Are you excited about all the room you have in the White House? I know that's the one thing that would get me there in a heartbeat! I hope you enjoy living there.

Thank you for taking the time to read my letter and thank you for trying so hard and actually being elected the new president! I look forward to four years of you in office!

Sincerely,
Amie, age 11
West Linn, OR

Dear President Obama,

I know you are looking for a dog to go with you to the White House. I think you should get a Dalmatian. The reason you should get a Dalmatian is because they are fire dogs and if there were a fire, the dog could lead you out of the White House, but of course you would have to teach him.

Sincerely,
Spencer, age 9
Heber Springs, AR

Dear President Obama,
How are Your pupes
and Your girls?
How are Your Daughters?
Your girls are Pritey!
Love, Richard,
P.S.- Do you Have a Car?

Richard, age 6
Evanston, IL

Dear President Obama,

My name is Alexus. I live in Des Moines, IA. Iowa is a good place to live. I hope one day you and your family can come down here and visit everyone. How many states have you been in?

I am close to your daughter's age but I'm older. I am eleven years old. When your kids go to school, does a body guard stay with them? Because that would be fun. I would be popular if I was the president's daughter.

Thank you for reading my letter.

Sincerely,
Alexus, age 11
Des Moines, IA

CHAPTER 6

The Issue That Matters Most to Me Is...

Kids want to be taken seriously, especially when they sit down and take the time to write a letter to the president of the United States. Usually they care about the same issues that concern adults—the economy, the war, global warming, immigration, education...but from a child's unique perspective.

One thing that stood out in these letters is how often kids had intimate knowledge of the subject that was of most concern. The letters about the war in Iraq would mention a father, a neighbor, a cousin, or a family friend who had been on multiple tours of duty. The letters on the subject of immigration came from children of immigrants. And when children wrote to the president about the economy, it was with the worry that their parents might not be able to make ends meet. There are few abstractions here. It's all too real for these children.

That's not to say that these are all grim letters. Many are full of hope and wonder at the changes the future will bring. Not all the issues are of extreme importance; a few are, well, let's just say they're about things that only a child could dream up.

Dear President Obama,

I think Global Warming is the most immportant issue because it's happining quickly and is hitting every living thing. Someday I want to go to the Arctic and see a poler bear teaching her cubs to fish and know they ar'nt indangered.

Please stop building highwyas and look for alternitave energy. Do not drill for oil off the coast or in the wildlife refuge in Alaska. We ride our bikes to the farmer's market and other people can do stuff like that too.

Good luck being President!

Yours truly,
Eli, age 9
Columbia, MD

Dear President Barack Obama,

I am so glad to have you as a president. If you could, please stop war. I don't like to see people fighting or dying. Thank you for listening to my opinion.

From,
Jenna, age 9
Cherry Hill, N.J.

Dear President Obama:

I want to know how you feel about NASA's Constellation Program. I heard you were thinking about canceling it. Have you made up your mind? If I were you, I would not because: it would be cool to see humans on Mars + is there life on Mars!!! Please consider the Constellation Program for future space travel.

Sincerely,
Braden, age 8
(I'll be 9 in 16 days)
Austin, TX

Dear President Obama,

I'm concerned about this situation:
    KIDS RIGHTS!!!!!!!!!!!!!!!!!!!!!
    I understand that we can't drink or drive, but why can't we vote or participate in anything that the government tells us we're not allowed to do. It is very mean. I think that it is, well, in my mind, the words "age discrimination." What are you and everybody else going to do about this situation? I know you will try your best to fix it. I know you will be the best president ever!
    Good luck in the next four years.

Thanks,
Seth, age 11
Stillwater, OK

(and Sasha, and Malia)
(and the first lady)
Dear President-elect Obama,

I know that you will be a great president and a great change to our country! But, there are probably some things that our country needs to change, that you do not know (or remember) about.

My friends and I have one thing on our minds, that need to change. Animal Rights! For instance Chinchillas, we have had people signing petitions, giving us 25¢, 50¢, or 75¢ (small amounts of money) and collecting recyclable bottle wrappers to save them. Most of us are only 10 years old and need more help to save them, why? Chinchillas are small Fluffy animals who are being bread for their fur or being kept as pets. Most people don't need the fur coats or mittens that they are buying, but do it anyway. If a Chinchilla trys to live in the wild it will probably be captured and killed. We Need Your Help to not only save the Chinchillas, but all of the animals in the world, like abandoned and mistreated Dogs and Cats! HELP! Your citizen
10 year old
Emma

Emma, age 10
Darnestown, MD

Dear President Obama,

There are some problems I think you should look into. One is the economy. The auto shops are shutting down. Another one is the poor. They are getting poorer. These are some problems.

Here is my advice for solving these problems. To help the economy you may want to make recycling a law. To help the poor, you could give them a job. That is my advice.

I have some questions that I want you to answer. My first question is, Did you want to be president when you were growing up? My last question is what was your childhood like? Please write back with your answers.

It is time to say good-bye. It's an honor to write to you and I will write to you again.

Your friend,
Cheyenne, age 11
Anderson, S.C.

Dear President Obama,

Here are some issues that I think should be fixed. First, I believe that kids should have gym everyday because kids don't get enough exercise, which is not healthy. Second, I think that every building in the United States should be smoke-free because when people smoke it can hurt them and also other people around them. Also, I don't think that there should be commercials for violent movies and TV shows on during sporting events on television because many kids just like me watch sporting events and that can plant violent things in their minds.

Next, I think that tickets to NFL games should not be so expensive because there are many diehard fans out there who love their team but cannot afford to go watch them play. Also I think that women's basketball players should get paid the same salary as the men. I think this because they do the same job and are just as athletic and some are even better.

Thank you for taking your time to read this and I hope you will consider my suggestions.

> Sincerely,
> Carolina, age 10
> Blue Bell, PA

Dear President Obama,

My grandmother died of cancer this past year and I have been waiting for a cure ever since she was diagnosed. I hope that one day I will be able to find it myself. Mr. President, could we give some of our money to cancer research programs? I think I have said what needs to be said.

Thank you for reading this (if you did) and I hope you will not be afraid to take advice from an eleven year old.

> Thanks ☺
> Emily, age 11
> Doylestown, PA

Dear Mr. President obama

My name is Rebeka and I am in Second Grade. I am happy that you are going to be our President. I Would like gas prices to go down because sometimes people don't Want to spend that much money on gas. There should be more food for the homeless people and money for them too. Homeless Shelters should have teachers for the adults who didn't have teachers, and for the kids who live thare and don't have school. There should be more Jobs and not as many lay-offs because sometimes this is something that second graders Worry about. Our country should be more friendly to animals like not building on the animal's habitat. I know you are going t take good care of our country.

Rebeka, 8 years old

Rebeka, age 8
Acton, MA

Dear President Obama,

I think you should try to save endangered animals, like the Blue Whale and the Mongolian Wild Pony. What is your favorite animal? Who was your favorite president?

I enjoy drawing and horseback riding and my favorite president is you and Theodore Roosevelt.

Good luck!

Sincerely,
Julia, age 9
Silver Spring, MD

Dear President Obama,

One issue that is important to me is how the world sees us. I think that if you do a few things like stop our independence on foreign countries, our image would improve.

Sincerely,
Asa, age 13
Sharon, VT

Dear mister President,

We want you to be the new President because we are excited about a black president. And not only because of that, with your help we can save the world from nature disaster and the ozone problems.

You can make sure that nobody will ever be slave again and that there will be no more wars.

We know you can do that.
We believe in you.

> Charis, age 10, and
> Katiana, age 8
> Zakynthos, Greece

Dear President Obama,

My name is Katie and I am five years old. I would like to know if you can cut taxes and save our environment. We need to protect our trees, we already have enough toilet paper. I would like to grow up and be President one day and be an airplane pilot too. Do you think I can do both?

Thank you for being our President.

> Sincerely,
> Katie, age 5
> Glen Burnie, MD

Dear President Obama,

I was thinking that you might want to stop tobacco production because some people just can't stop smoking!

In my opinion you should make zoos have open cages and put the animals in open areas with boundaries and give them more and better food, along with playmates.

> Sincerely,
> Mason, age 11
> Stillwater, OK

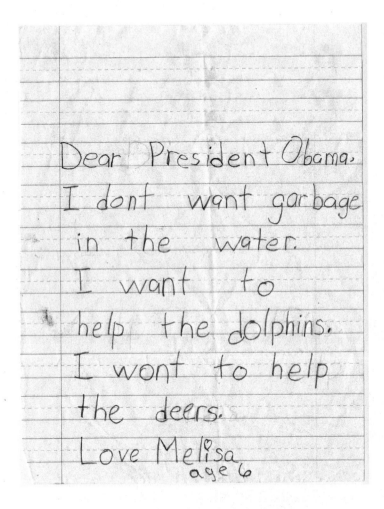

Dear President Obama,
I dont want garbage in the water.
I want to help the dolphins.
I wont to help the deers.
Love Melisa
age 6

Melisa, age 6
Greenlawn, N.Y.

Dear President Obama,

While you are in office, I would like you to make it easier for middle class families to pay for college. I know I am only 13 years old, but I am already very worried about my future.

My sister, Hannah, received very good grades in school and is a very talented dancer. She was accepted into Dickinson, Bryn Mawr, Haverford, and other fine colleges. But my family cannot afford to send her to any of these colleges. She won partial scholarships, but the cost of tuition is so high, her awards were not nearly enough.

I understand that your first priority in office is to fix the economy in ways that make sure people have homes to live in and food to eat. But please try to find a way for families like mine to give their smart, hardworking, children a good education so they can become a generation America is proud of.

Sincerely,
Sarah, age 13
Columbia, MD

Dear President Obama,

I would appreciate it if you would raise the salary for educators. They work extremely hard and without them, we wouldn't have great leaders like you. Teachers help us become great. I would appreciate it if you would give this some thought.

> Your new friend,
> Jordan, age 11
> Layton, UT

Dear President Obama,

I hope you don't have any trouble moving into the White House.

I hope you make ATM machines accessible for people in wheelchairs, because that's really hard for me.

I hope you make the war in Israel be over immediately when you become president. I don't mean to be rude here, but if you don't, I might not get my first chance to go to Israel for our friend's son's Bar Mitzvah in April.

I congratulate you on being the first African American president of the United States. I wish that after four years, you win again. I hope everybody in the world—Democrats, Republicans, blacks, whites, Asians, Hispanic, Persian, Korean, gay, Christian, Jewish, Mormon, Catholic, Muslim— votes for you.

I really think if you have everybody in the world looking to you to fix all the problems, that will be a lot of pressure—not only for you, but for your family and, I hate to say it, the Secret Service. Look to your First Lady a lot— she can help you make decisions.

> Yours sincerely,
> Ezra, age 13
> Los Angeles, CA

Dear Mr. President,

There are a lot of things I think should be done to help our country out. One important thing is to help people out who don't have the money to take their children to the dentist or the doctor, or to even take themselves. I think it is terrible for kids to either be sick or have a bad toothache and their parents can't afford to take them to the dentist or the doctor. I also know that people are having a hard time finding jobs that you can make enough money to live on. Everything costs so much money now.

I hope you enjoy living in the White House and can do things to help our country. By the way, how would you feel if you had not won the election?

> Sincerely,
> Brittany, age 11
> West Linn, OR

Dear President Obama,

How does it feel to be President? I bet it feels AWESOME!!!

Anyway, would you make smoking illegal, especially when there are kids in the home or vehicle? My mom and dad smoke, so I just wondered.

Thank you for your time.

> Sincerely yours truly,
> Hannah, age 11
> Stillwater, OK

Dear Barack Obama

Hello My name is Keely
I don't think you
should take away gun rights
because we might need
them for protesion one day.
We also need to get
this econimy under control.

I am going to stop complaning
now and say "Congradulsion"
on wining the election!

From: Keely

Keely, age 11
Stillwater, OK

Dear President Obama,

Hello, I am a 5th grader who feels strongly about the gun control crisis. What will you do about the current gun control crisis going on in the United States? I suggest having weapon owners submit to tests to see if they are fit to carry weapons. The tests should be held in buildings called DGWs which stands for "Department of Guns and Weapons." I have one question that I made for the test: "Do you have any problems that interfere with your ability to aim a weapon? If so list them here." Anyway you should have weapon owners submit to tests to see if they are fit to carry guns. I hope you can find some ideas for resolving the gun control crisis!

Sincerely,
Corwin, age 10
Newport News, VA

Dear President Obama,

I know you're busy but I need to ask you some questions. Before I get into the questions, I hope you don't think this is just another letter from a 10-year-old boy, because I'm really thoughtful.

Since you're president of the United States, what are you going to do about the littering and the trash in the oceans? About the construction workers cutting down the trees? They're killing the animals and polluting the air. I'm telling you this because where I live, there's a lot of wood buildings—and they're still building!

I think you are going to be a good president. I wonder how it feels to be the first black president of the United States.

You can find me in Virginia at my school or at [home address].

Sincerely,
Jhymon, age 10
Newport News, VA

P.S. Good luck on the presidency job.

Dear President Obama,

My name is Imanne. My family of five and I live in Berkeley, California. I am in third grade.

I think that you have a chance to improve the United States. Many schools in America are not doing very well. Children are not getting a proper education.

I also think you should do something about alcohol and drugs. Many people are getting addicted to them. People are going crazy and doing things that they wouldn't have done before.

Please think about what I said and consider doing something about it.

Sincerely,
Imanne, age 8
Berkeley, CA

Dear President Obama,

I want you to think about helping nature because nature is what we live on, and without nature we wouldn't be here. People have been cutting down rainforests just to get a better crop. However, the cutting down of the rainforest is killing all kinds of species of animals! Like the Sumatran tiger and orangutan that live in rainforests are now nearly extinct. I would like you to try to change the way people think about the rainforest, and the animals in it. It would mean a lot to me, and other people.

Love,
Camille, age 8
Overland Park, KS

Dear President Obama,

You probably don't need help from a ten-year-old, but these are the things I think you should change. I think we should use more wind energy. I also think we should take our troops out of Iraq. I think we should have more nature preserves and people should stop cutting down trees and be nicer to our environment; we only have 1 world. I also think everyone should have health care, and should go to whatever school they want.

Sincerely,
Natalie, age 10
Centerport, N.Y.

Dear President Obama,

Hi, my name is Olga. How are you? Well I'm just fine. I hope that you are fine too, because now you will need it more than ever. I am very glad that you won the elections. I am very proud of you that you stopped smoking.

I would be very thankfuly with you if you would fix the immigration problem. First of all, I know that there are alot of other problems, but I'm really interested in the immigration problem. I've seen alot of people suffering, on the news because they've been deported back to their country.

Whenever I hear of people being deported, I start crying, because I don't have both of my parents living with me. I have to wait every week for the phone to ring and hear my mom's voice. I need to hear her voice to see if she's fine.

I hope you can fix this problem, and THANK YOU for taking some of your important minutes to read my letter.

Respectfully,
Olga
I'm 12 yrs. old.

Olga, age 12
Fort Worth, TX

Dear President Obama,

I wonder if you know about problems in the U.S. . . . such as people losing their jobs or being unemployed. Some of the people—aunts, uncles, and older cousins—can't feed their children because they don't have a job. How are they going to pay their bills? Here's a problem I'm going to tell you now, which is the stock market crashing. That's a major problem, because people are using up America's money. I hope you can solve some of these major problems.

Anyway! Congrats on becoming the President of the U.S.

> One of your
> voter's son,
> Antonio, age 11
> Anderson, S.C.

Dear President Obama,

I'm writing to you because of a problem, the immigrants we have here in America. Most immigrants came here for a better life and to have a better living. They need legal documentation to do that. That's why I'm writing to you. There are many hard working immigrants here. Some families get separated when the police catch them and then send them back to their country. To me that is very melancholy. How would you feel if your parents and family members were immigrants and they were taken? You would feel lonely, right? What is your plan for immigrants and how will it help them? A suggestion would be to give immigrants legal documentation.

Good luck and please write back.

Sincerely,
Dennis, age 11
Silver Spring, MD

Dear President Obama,

Hi, I'm Kate. I know you will be a great president who will be able to keep our country safe. As president, you may want to make some changes. An example could be drinking. I think there should be bigger consequences for drunk driving. I know how dangerous drunk driving is for the person and anyone around them, but I think they should enforce the law better. I lost my cousin because of a drunk driver and I know how it feels to lose someone you love.

Please think about some changes because America is absolutely ready for a change.

Thanks—
Kate, age 11
Doylestown, PA

Dear President Obama,

I am a girl living in a rural Vermont town. I consider myself lucky compared to many, but a small fear weaves its way into my mind as I learn more about earth's current situation, global warming. I hope that you as president will take the time to consider the current generation and what kind of world we will grow up and live and work in. I am curious and a tad frightened as to what the future I am heading toward may hold. Will the generations following ours get to experience what we have now? A real winter in Vermont? Ski down its slopes? Learn about diverse species *that still exist?* Or only exist as relics of the past? I hope that you, as president, will take the time to reflect on the future of your daughters and other children of this nation.

Sincerely,
Lucyanna, age 13
Stockbridge, VT

Dear President Barack Obama,

Please stop the war in Iraq and Afghanistan. My favorite uncle is going to Afghanistan. I want him to come home safe. I collected toys and crafts to send to children in Afghanistan.

I was so happy when you won President of the United States. Thank you for reading my letter.

Your friend,
Sabrina, age 8
Hyde Park, N.Y.

Dear President Obama,

Thank you for getting elected; I have no doubt that you will be one of the greatest presidents ever. I am a 6th grade student in Layta, UT, USA Earth, solar system, Orion spur, Milkey way, local group, universe 1. I know this is not one of the most urgent problems facing our country, but I believe that you should put some funding into astrophysics, NASA, and molecular physics. For these reasons: to enhanse understanding of the universe, to find other habitable planets, and to solve why the Big Bang happed and the nano-seconds after it. My dad and I are both avid 'all around' science readers. Last year (2008) we did a science project showing the gravity does not pull, it's the bending of space-time pushing things tward the center of mass. If you could make this type of science mandatory in school I would be very great ful.

Sincerely, Connor   age 12

Connor, age 12
Layton, UT

Dear President Obama,

My name is Yonah. These are my opinions on how to run the country. I think that you should keep the soldiers in Iraq. If you take some out, the rest will die. If you take them out, the Iraqi soldiers will go to Israel or a country nearby. If you raise taxes, it will affect me and everyone else.

You should ask McCain if he has any opinions because he had some good ideas.

Sincerely
Yonah, age 9
Rochester, N.Y.

Dear President Obama,

I have an issue to complain about. My stepdad is in the army and he misses out on the holidays that everyone else celebrates. I just wanted to say that can you please switch when they go to Iraq to a different day that is NOT close to the holidays please. There is another issue I have. It has to do with the terrorism. I did not like it when the terrorists bombed the Twin Towers. I had a relative that died in the bomb incident! If you can, can you stop this? It's driving me crazy! Thank you very much.

Sincerely,
Caitlyn, age 11
Newport News, VA

Dear President Obama,

Could you stop the war in Iraq? Because my dad is going on a lot of TDYs [temporary duty assignments] and travels to Iraq and I don't get to see him that much. It's been about five years that the war has been going on, and it's too hard on the military people. I was just wondering if you could please do that.

Anyway, good luck on being the president!

Sincerely,
Ashlee, age 11
Clearfield, UT

CHAPTER 7

Oh, and One More Thing, Mr. President!

This chapter is comprised of all the random ideas that kids come up with—the stuff that's impossible to categorize that leaves you amazed by the boundless curiosity, candor, and utter unpredictability of children. There are suggestions for what the First Family should do with their free time, questions about their private lives, imaginative wishes for the future, plus a couple of Obama-inspired poems, and even a knock-knock joke.

Wouldn't it be great if the president could really do all the magical things the kids suggested? Well, maybe not *everything:* If he really did make it rain bubble gum, that would just dent our cars and get stuck all over everything.

Even though he's already secured his place in history, if Barack Obama could accomplish just one or two of the astonishing things these kids suggest, he really would be the greatest president of all time!

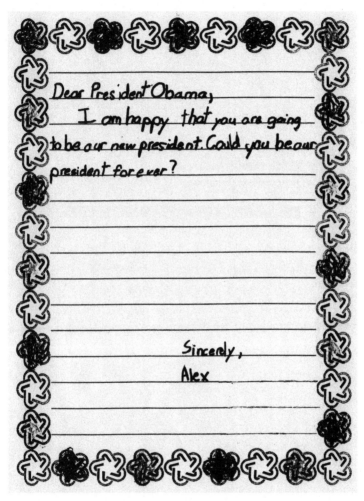

Dear President Obama,
    I am happy that you are going to be our new president. Could you be our president forever?

                    Sincerly,
                    Alex

Alex, age 7
Glendale, CA

Dear President Obama,

You can get everything you want. You should bring a yo-yo to the White House.

> Sincerely,
> Thai, age 9
> St. Louis, MO

Dear President Obama,

I have a bunny. I think you are really smart. Also, I think you are as sweet as cake.

> Yours truly,
> Jendy, age 9
> Skokie, IL

Dear President,

My name is Kaitlyn and I am 7 years old. Why are there no girl presidents? I will try to be a president someday if my mom lets me. But if she says no, I will try to do something else.

It is important to be a president. I bet you're kind of happy that you are the president, and a nice president. I will try to be the president someday if I can be the president.

> Kaitlyn, age 7
> Hyde Park, N.Y.

Dear President Obama,

I love you, Obama. I want you to come over and watch my brother Ben play his guitar and his drums and maybe you could play a guitar too.

I feel good that you're the president and I hope you'll say good things and do good things for the whole wide world. You should ask people to do good things and things that are right and I want you to be good for the whole wide world like being nice and doing things that are nice for people that love you and I'm glad you are the president because I really wanted you to be the president because I really like you and I want you to play with us one day.

I want you to be the president for every world.

> Ellie, age 4³/₄
> Washington, D.C.

Dear Mr. President Obama,

I love writing. I want to ask you, when's your birthday? I need to tell you that my birthday is January 20. Can I come to your party?

It's an honor to write to you. YOU RULE!

> Sincerely, with hope,
> Lexi, age 9
> Downingtown, PA

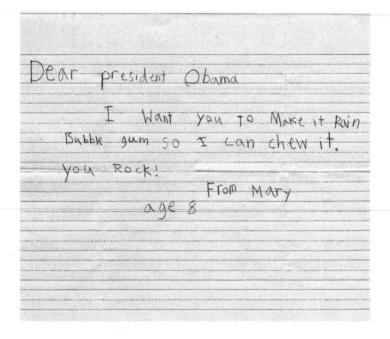

Dear president Obama

I Want you to Make it Rain Bubble gum so I can chew it.

you Rock!

From Mary
age 8

Mary, age 8
Washington, D.C.

Dear President Obama,

Here's a poem I wrote about you. I hope you like it.
   "Barack Obama in the White House"

   Barack Obama in the White House in the Ice House
   Chillin' with his daughters and his wife.
   John McCain, losing by far, snoozing in his car.
   Barack Obama and his family, having fun in the
       White House.

                              Love,
                              Steven, age 6
                              Washington, D.C.

Dear President Obama,

I feel excited because you are President. The best part will
be when you ride the Air Force One. You should bring a
dog and paperwork.

                              Sincerely,
                              Everette, age 9
                              St. Louis, MO

Dear President Obama,

My favorite super hero is Spiderman. I think it is neat that
he gets to use his webs to climb buildings and help catch
the bad guys. I like Batman too but he cannot swing

through the air like Spiderman. When you were a kid like me, who was your favorite super hero?

Eamon, age 6
Silver Spring, MD

Dear President Obama,

When you become president, do you still get to talk to your friends or do you have to make all new ones? I was wondering because I know security is pretty tight. If you do not get to talk to your friends anymore, I feel sorry for you. Are you still able to go out whenever you want? If so, I bet it gets annoying with all the people coming up to you now that you are famous, demanding your autograph. If you do not get out, I bet it gets boring just staying there in the White House. You might even be able to go out and have a family night and watch a movie every once in a while.

Well, I am sure you have business to do, so I will stop here.

Sincerely,
Elissa, age 9
Knox City, TX

Dear Mr Obama,:
I am glad your gotta be the
our 44th President. Mommy said It's
going to be colder. You need
to wear a hat and gloves ard
hat and scarfs. You. don't like
to be like William Henry Harrison
died of Hiperpermia and please.
stop smoking. You should please.
have a Pertuges with a dog. My
cousin's dog is scottie he
he. is so cute. We are planing to
going to Washington. DC to see
the Lincoln Memorial, Jefferson
Memorial, The White house I'll shake
your hand

From,
Jeffrey

Jeffrey, age 8
Branchburg, N.J.

Dear President Obama,

How is the experience of being president so far? Is it good or bad for you? If I were president, my daily experience would be horrible. The world would be crashing down all around me. (I know nothing of being the president.) Now that you are president, the world is safe from me. Haha. My other question is, Is it hard to talk people into voting for you? I would be scared they would tell me to my face that they would vote, and then behind my back not vote for me. I hope you have a swell experience of being President.

Respectfully yours,
Hayden, age 9
Knox City, TX

Dear President Obama,

Can I please tell you an Obama joke?

Knock, knock.
Who's there?
Obama.
Obama who?
Obama You!

I want you to lift weights to be strong. I want you to come to my school so my friends can meet you.

Love,
Nate, age 5
Atlanta, GA

Dear President Obama,

We have two chess players at my school (including me) that want to see how good you are. Can you make a chess game on your website? Then we can play over the Internet with you.

Sincerely,
Ijaaz, age 11
Bloomfield, CT

Dear President Obama,

I heard that you are a big sports fan like me, and your favorite team is the Chicago White Sox. Mine is the Mets. I thought it was funny when at a press conference you made the reporters sit on the Cubs side and the White Sox side.

My favorite president was Teddy Roosevelt. I hope you are like him. He was also a sports fan but he liked football best.

Good luck for the next four years.

From,
Paul, age 7½
Fort Salonga, N.Y.

Barack,

My family and I are thrilled with excitement that you won,
We will cry when your job as president is done.

O h, President Obama, I know you will do your
new job with great responsibility,
Make sure your daughters, Sasha and Melia
enjoy and take care of their new puppy.

B arack, thank you for making children one of
your priorities,
With you as our new president, we're one of
the luckiest of countries!

A thank you to you for promising to stop the war
in Iraq,
Please try your personal best, President Barack.

M y class election was rewarding, though when I
ran for President I didn't make it,
However I was chosen to be our Ambassador of
Friendship!

A last chance to say thank you for running for our
USA president,
I know a majority of the people chose wisely
and were never hesitant!

Your #1 Fan,
Calista, age 8
Castaic, CA

Dear Mr. President,

I heard you play baseball. I could play you one day, and if I won, I could say I beat the President of the United States.
    Best of luck, you will need it.

Sincerely,
Will, age 12
West Linn, OR

Dear Mr. President,

If I was your son I would be running around with all the toys I would have. And be running around again. And I would tell my friends and everyone I know. But that would happen if I were your son, which I am not.
    Oh, I forgot to tell you my name is Kristopher but you can call me Kris. When I grow up I want to be a stuntman. I am in 5th grade.

With respect,
Kristopher, age 11
Sherman Oaks, CA

Hello President Obama,

Have you ever met any superstars on TV like the Jonas Brothers (Joe, Kevin or Nick) or Demi Lovato, or The Rock?

From,
Tony, age 10
Studio City, CA

Dear President Obama,

I was so happy when you got elected. I have written you a poem.

    *Because you're **B**est*
    *Because you're **A**wesome*
    *Because you're **R**adical*
    *Because you're **A**mazing*
    *Because you're **C**ool*
    *Because you're **K**ind*

    *Because you're **O**utstanding*
    *Because you're **B**lazing*
    *Because you're **A**dmirable*
    *Because you're **M**arvelous*
    *Because you're **A**stonishing*

> Good luck,
> Davin, age 11
> Fairfield, IA

Dear Mr. Obama,

I saw you on TV and I was so happy you won, I jumped up and down. In fact, I was so happy I told my mom and she was happy, too. So we went to my grandma's house. My grandma already knew you had won. She was cooking some steak and potatoes, green beans, and cornbread.

I am your number one fan because you are the first black president in America. I am just so proud of you. If you have time, could you read my letter on the news?

From,
Alyncia, age 10
St. Louis, MO

Dear President Obama,

Are you still John McCain's friend after all the debates? If you are, could you tell him I said hello?

I was wondering if you might consider lowering taxes on items our parents might buy. If you could do this, kids could get more presents during birthdays and Christmas. I know you can do this because you are the best president ever. I will say my please and thank you in advance!

Your grateful citizen,
Tyler, age 9
Knox City, TX

Dear President Obama,

I am glad you are on TV every day. I know you wear a tie all the time. I know you love God. Everybody loves God. How is your day as a president? Do you have time to spend with your family? Would you like to come to Seattle and meet my mommy?

Jessy, age 6
Lynnwood, WA

Dear President Obama,

I think it will be the best living in the White House and having a butler.

I am concerned about some classrooms being dirty. I think to change it, you should send letters to all of the schools and tell them to clean them more.

Sincerely,
Janae, age 9
St. Louis, MO

Dear President Obama,

I am an artist. You should have art around because it helps you think. Mr. President, I have one question, how long did it take you to learn how to read? My letters are easy but sometimes it takes me a long time to read them all together. I am glad you are president, did I tell you that already?

Do a great job. I will pray for you.

Future voter,
Shalom, age 6
Indianapolis, IN

P.S. I think Sasha is really cute.

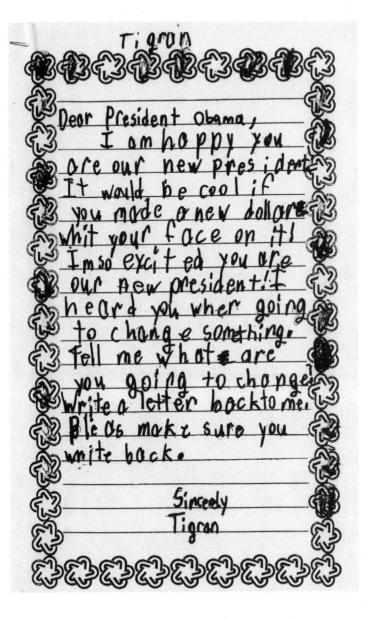

Tigran

Dear President Obama,
 I am happy you
are our new president.
It would be cool if
you made a new dollar
whit your face on it!
Im so excited you are
our new president! I
heard you wher going
to change something.
Tell me what are
you going to change!
Write a letter backto me.
Pleas makle sure you
write back.

Sincerly
Tigran

Tigran, age 7
Glendale, CA

Dear President Obama,

On this show called *Oprah* there was a little boy who said you would succeed in making gas money available for us car drivers. Well, technically not me, but my mom and dad.

Everyone who comes to my house (trust me, that's a lot of people!) wanted you to win!

We love you,
Julius, age 9
Skokie, IL

Dear President Orack Obama,

I love that you are the president of the United States of America. I will vote for you when I turn 18 years old. I love you!

I wrote the following song for you which I sing while marching holding the flag of the United States of America.

I love Orack Obama,
I love Orack Obama,
I love Orack Obama.
Orack Obama

XOXO,
Alexandra, age 5
Adamstown, MD

ACKNOWLEDGMENTS

Thanks are due to Pamela Cannon for her unerring editorial judgment; and to Jeanne Welsh, Peggy Robin, Karen Adler, and Claire Adler for collecting, cataloging, and reviewing the two-thousand-plus letters from children from all corners of the country and from many foreign lands. Mel Berger was invaluable in getting this project started and seeing it through to its conclusion.

We wish we could thank all the children by name who took the time to write a letter to the president and send us a copy for publication in this book. Alas, we do not have the space for that, but we hope that this note of thanks will be read by everyone who sent in letters, especially those who wrote wonderfully imaginative letters that, for one reason or another—such as many letters from the same small town—we did not include in this collection.

Fortunately, we do have space to list all the teachers and parents who collected letters from students in schools, clubs, and service organizations. In alphabetical order, we send a big thank-you to:

Barton Hills Elementary School, Austin, TX, letters from Ms. Jaynes's 3rd grade, sent in by parent Sara Hickman.

Beverly J. Martin Elementary School, Ithaca, N.Y., sent in by Ms. Salamon.

Capital City Public Charter School, Washington, D.C., sent in by Ms. Robin's 7th and 8th grade.

Castaic Elementary School, Castaic, CA, sent in by Ms. Abramson and Ms. Ashley.

Chaparral Elementary School, Calabasas, CA, sent in by Mrs. Shipow.

Charles E. Smith Jewish Day School, Rockville, MD, sent in by Ms. Weissman.

Cold Spring Elementary School, Doylestown, PA, sent in by Ms. Silver's and Mrs. Schmidt's 6th grade.

Dewey Elementary School, Evanston, IL, sent in without a teacher's note.

Dixie Canyon Elementary School, Sherman Oaks, CA, sent in by Ms. Cannon's 2nd grade and Ms. Boccalatte's 5th grade.

Dixon Middle School, Provo, UT, sent in by Ms. Moody.

Edgerton Community School, Edgerton, WI, sent in by Ms. Fox.

Forest View Elementary School, Everett, WA, sent in by Ms. Henderson and Ms. Davis.

G-Men Young Men's Group, Greenwood Baptist Church, Brooklyn, N.Y., sent in by Mr. Stringfellow.

Girl Scout Troop 91176 of Greater Philadelphia, PA, sent in by Ms. Butler, Assistant Troop Leader.

Heber Springs Elementary School, Heber Springs, AR, sent in by Mrs. Kemp's 3rd grade.

Hillel Community Day School, Rochester, N.Y., sent in by Ms. Kantor.

Hoosick Falls Elementary School, Hoosick Falls, N.Y., sent in by Mrs. Burdick's 3rd grade.

ILM Tree Co-op School, Lafayette, CA, sent in by Ms. Ali.

Imagine Charter School of Broward, Coral Springs, FL, sent in without a teacher's note.

Jefferson School, Bergenfield, N.J., sent in by Ms. Rossi and Ms. Vogel.

John Muir Elementary School, Santa Monica, CA, sent in by Ms. Vallejo's 1st grade.

Kirkbride Elementary School, Philadelphia, PA, sent in by Ms. Visco's 2nd grade.

Knox City Elementary School, Knox City, TX, sent in by Ms. Baker-Adkins's 4th grade.

Kyrene del Norte Elementary School, Tempe, AZ, sent in by Ms. Robertson.

Lakeside Middle School, Anderson, S.C., sent in without a teacher's note.

Lee Hall Elementary School, Newport News, VA, sent in by Ms. Haghparast's 5th grade.

Love of Learning Montessori School, Centerport, N.Y., sent in with a note signed simply "From the teachers at Love of Learning Montessori School."

Mann Elementary School's One on One INSPIRE Program, St. Louis, MO, sent in by Ms. Knights.

Marymount International School, Rome, Italy, sent in by Ms. Gallagher, teacher of the 4th grade English as a Second Language class.

Mountain View Elementary School, Layton, UT, letters from Ms. Appleby's 6th grade, sent in by parent volunteer Susan Zeller Smith.

Netherwood Elementary School, Hyde Park, N.Y., sent in by Ms. Miller, Ms. Walsh, and Ms. Cameron, co-teachers of 1st and 2nd grades.

No. 23 School, and No. 36 School, Rochester, N.Y., sent in by literacy volunteer Jan Feldman.

Oak View Elementary School, Silver Spring, MD, letters from the Oak View Dragons (they wanted it noted!) sent in by Mrs. Seitzel and Mrs. Turner.

R.D. White Elementary School, Glendale, CA, sent in by Ms. Casciani, Ms. Thorpe, Ms. Holland, Mrs. Svab, and Ms. Junge.

Raymond Case Elementary School, Elk Grove, CA, sent in by Ms. Baeta.

River Woods Elementary School, Des Moines, IA, sent in by Ms. Peters's 4th and 5th grade special education class.

Riverside Middle School's AVID Program, Fort Worth, TX, sent in by Ms. Turner.

Robinwood Elementary School, Florissant, MO, sent in by Mr. Linenfelser.

Rosemont Ridge Middle School, West Linn, OR, sent in by Mr. Snook and Mrs. Cronn, teachers of the 6th grade.

Sai Brindavan Centre, Coconut Grove, Puttaparthi, India, sent in by Mrs. Raghavan and Ms. Laksmi.

Sharon Academy, Sharon, VT, sent in by Ms. Innes's 7th and 8th grade.

Sprouts of Hope, Cambridge, MA chapter of Roots & Shoots, Jane Goodall's environmental action group, sent in by Ms. Ludtke.

Stillwater Middle School, Stillwater, OK, sent in by Mr. Baldwin's 6th grade.

Tanaina Elementary School, Wasilla, AK, sent in by Ms. Johnson's 5th grade.

Walker School, Evanston, IL, sent in by Ms. Rosenbluh's 4th grade and Ms. Slattery's 1st grade.

Our sincere apologies to anyone
we may have inadvertently left out!

*A Short Gide to Undrstanding
the Kreative Spelings That Kidz Used*

CREATIVE SPELLING	ORDINARY SPELLING
alternitave	*alternative*
ar'nt	*aren't*
bak	*back*
birther	*birthday*
Brokle	*broccoli*
Calafornya	*California*
child hod	*childhood*
cinde	*kind*
cline	*clean*
coligreens	*collard greens*
conchrey	*country*
congojalashens	*congratulations*
congraltans	*congratulations*
congrgelusion	*congratulations*
cris mis	*Christmas*
desition	*decision*

dotters	*daughters*
econimical	*economic*
eletion	*election*
faveret	*favorite*
favorit	*favorite*
gode	*good*
goodest	*best*
gowing	*going*
happining	*happening*
holaday	*holiday*
houndsom	*handsome*
immmportant	*important*
indangered	*endangered*
kertusy	*courtesy*
kined	*kind*
letol	*little*
lettering	*littering*
litterring	*littering*
luke	*luck*
mett	*meet*
mogle	*mogul*
mostest	*the most*
musick	*music*
necxt	*next*
numbr	*number*
Orack	*Barack*
plese	*please*
pleys	*please*
poler bear	*polar bear*
presedent	*president*
pritey	*pretty*

protcsion	*protection*
pupes	*puppies*
puppys	*puppies*
realy	*really*
respeckt	*respect*
rite	*write*
seckent	*second*
sere	*sure*
shod	*should*
siyents	*science*
taxs	*taxes*
wan't	*want*
wat	*what*
wite house	*White House*
wrting	*writing*
yers	*years*

ABOUT THE EDITORS

BILL ADLER is a literary agent and the author of numerous books, including several *New York Times* bestsellers, and #1 bestsellers. He created the Kids' Letters series of books, which has included *Kids' Letters to President Kennedy* and *Letters from Camp.* He lives in New York City.

BILL ADLER, JR. is the author of more than twenty books, including *Outwitting Squirrels* and *Kids' E-mails and Letters from Camp.* He lives in Washington, D.C.

Between them, father and son have written more than sixty titles on topics ranging from humor and politics to sports, history, and science.